COUNCIL *on*
FOREIGN
RELATIONS

Center for Preventive Action

I0122069

Discussion Paper
December 2019

Preparing for the Next Foreign Policy Crisis

What the United States Should Do

Paul B. Stares

CONTENTS

PREPARING FOR THE NEXT FOREIGN POLICY CRISIS
What the United States Should Do

Paul B. Stares

Managing foreign policy crises has become a recurring challenge for U.S. presidents. Since the end of the Cold War, there have been one hundred twenty occasions in which a threatening development overseas triggered a period of intense, high-level deliberation about what the United States should do in response (see the list of U.S. foreign policy crises from 1989 to 2019, pages 18–23 in this report).[1] This equates to an average of fifteen crises for each four-year presidential term. Although the stakes varied from crisis to crisis, each required the president to decide—usually in pressured circumstances and with considerable uncertainty about the risks involved—whether the situation warranted sending military forces in harm's way to protect U.S. interests. On more than forty occasions, the president determined that it did. While most of these crises were eventually resolved with little or no lasting impact on U.S. interests, some festered and became more difficult and costly to address at a later date.[2] Not surprisingly, former presidents and their senior advisors have often looked back at a particular crisis with regret at some of the choices that were made.[3]

It is unlikely that foreign policy crises will become any less frequent or vexing for future U.S. presidents. The signs all point in the opposite direction. By most appraisals, the world is entering a more turbulent and crisis-prone era.[4] Recent actions by the United States, particularly by the Donald J. Trump administration, have contributed to this turbulence as well as to the perception that the United States may no longer be as committed to playing an active role in some regions.[5] Such uncertainty could encourage some states and actors to test the United States' resolve; others, hedging against U.S. disengagement, could adopt policies that are inadvertently destabilizing.

The most worrisome challenge for the United States in the future would be a crisis involving another major power, risking military escalation and even war. Such confrontations have become more likely in recent years as U.S. relations with China and Russia have deteriorated and tensions have risen in several disputed areas. A serious U.S. confrontation with either power would at the least deepen mutual mistrust and animosity, just as similar crises did in the early days of the Cold War. This outcome would have profound implications for world order, particularly on the prospects for cooperation on pressing global challenges such as climate change, nuclear proliferation, and public health threats.

The risk that relatively localized events overseas could rapidly expand into much larger, even global, emergencies is also increasing.[6] The world's primary operating systems are now so tightly coupled that even relatively minor disruptions or shocks from geopolitical events are likely to reverberate widely and rapidly. The 2014 Ebola outbreak in West Africa, for example, precipitated emergency precautions as far away as the United States following reports of infected individuals entering the country. Similarly, the 2017 WannaCry ransomware cyberattack that eventually affected computers in one hundred fifty countries illustrates how a relatively discrete event can escalate in a harmful and unpredictable way. Preparing for and managing these disruptions before they unleash a dangerous chain reaction has thus become a real concern for U.S. policymakers.

It is vital, therefore, that the United States devote more attention and resources to preventing potential crises from arising and being better prepared to manage them when they do. For the last ten years, the Center for Preventive Action (CPA) at the Council on Foreign Relations has closely studied how the United States can accomplish this task. This report represents a distillation of CPA's findings and recommendations. It is organized into three parts: The first discusses the core challenge that U.S. policymakers face in trying to be better prepared to manage foreign policy crises. The second lays out a variety of ways in which this challenge can be overcome to improve U.S. preparedness for future crises. The third offers specific institutional recommendations.

BACKGROUND

From the earliest days of the republic, U.S. presidents have had to grapple with foreign policy crises.[7] However, it was not until the twentieth century—and particularly after World War II, when the United States became a global power with global commitments—that foreign policy crises posed a regular and serious challenge to U.S. presidents. While the stakes subsided considerably with the end of the Cold War, the frequency of foreign policy crises has not. Crisis management has become an almost constant preoccupation for senior U.S. officials.

U.S. policymakers can hedge against the risks of a more turbulent and crisis-prone world in two ways. One would be for the United States to substantially increase its military power both to deter aggressors or opportunists and to have more capabilities to protect U.S. interests when crises erupt. Alternatively, the United States could recalibrate its foreign policy interests and reduce its commitments around the world to lessen its exposure to threatening developments overseas.[8] After all, a crisis is only a crisis if U.S. interests or values are considered imperiled.

Neither of these strategies, however, is likely to affect the number of crises the United States faces. They could also make matters worse. U.S. military superiority after the Cold War did little, if anything, to lessen the frequency of crises or ease the challenge they posed to U.S. presidents. Increasing U.S. military capabilities could also likely raise fears about U.S. intentions and conceivably trigger countervailing actions by other major powers. A broad strategy of global retrenchment by the United States, even if done with care, could likewise have unwelcome consequences. Revisionist powers and malign actors, for example, could take advantage of the vacuum left by a diminishing U.S. presence. America's allies and partners could at the same time grow more skeptical of U.S. defense guarantees and adopt policies intended to improve their own security but which could prove to be regionally destabilizing.[9]

The costs and risks associated with both of these strategies have typically led to a third option: a deliberate effort to provide U.S. presidents and senior officials with better warning of incipient crises so that they can either avert a crisis or respond more effectively. Virtually every U.S. administration—certainly those in recent years—has aspired to be more proactive about managing foreign policy crises.[10] Despite the best of intentions, however, U.S. policymakers continue to be surprised by threatening developments overseas, reacting in a belated and ad hoc fashion. This track record does not suggest that similar efforts in the future could produce better results. For this reason, a different approach is needed—one that first understands the nature of the challenge that policymakers face.

The 2009 Council Special Report *Enhancing U.S. Preventive Action* captured the core challenge facing any effort to improve U.S. crisis preparedness:

> Getting policymakers to commit resources proactively to address a hypothetical problem when there are demonstrably real ones in need of attention is difficult. Even when there are convincing signs of an emerging crisis, harried policymakers are still inclined to focus on managing the problem on their desks rather than the one still buried in their in-boxes. By the time the danger signals are unavoidable, the opportunities for early preventive action may have passed or the remaining options may seem either ineffective or too risky, further compounding the political inertia. This problem is especially evident when U.S. interests are seemingly not directly imperiled.[11]

The fixation on managing the present reinforces the tendency to ignore the future. This increases the likelihood that the United States will be blindsided by events overseas. Published in the wake of the Arab Spring, which had caught Washington completely unprepared, a 2011 CFR Policy Innovation Memorandum argued that there is little demand for forward-looking assessments since policymakers are primarily interested in short-term "current intelligence" to help them manage events that could occur next week rather than next year.[12] Since 9/11, the overwhelming priority of U.S. intelligence collection and analysis has been to warn of further terrorist attacks and to support the operational needs of U.S. forces in Afghanistan, Iraq, and other places around the world—all essentially near-term requirements. The upshot of this shortsightedness is that other than the annual unclassified global threat briefing by the director of national intelligence to Congress, there is no regular and systematic process of "scanning the horizon" for either potentially threatening developments or political opportunities that could arise.[13]

The same shortsightedness also means there is little incentive to carry out serious preparations to manage potential crises, much less think about how they might be averted. As the 2011 report observes:

> Busy policymakers are understandably reluctant to expend precious time on planning for potential crises that may

never materialize, especially those that seem particularly remote or seemingly inconsequential. With every crisis, there is also a natural resistance to make plans that may be irrelevant to the specific circumstances or quickly rendered meaningless. Policymakers also like to retain maximum freedom of maneuver in a crisis, which pre-planning threatens to restrict.[14]

As a result, aside from the regular military contingency planning by the Department of Defense and the preparations by the Department of Homeland Security to manage various catastrophic domestic events, there exists no routinized, government-wide policy planning effort focused on prospective foreign policy challenges.

Given the daily pressures that most senior officials face, there is likewise little appetite or opportunity to carry out pre-crisis exercises and simulations to familiarize officials and policymakers with emerging foreign policy problems or to rehearse procedures and test emergency systems. In particular, political appointees, who primarily occupy the senior crisis management positions in the U.S. government, receive little or no preparation for what they are likely to encounter while in office.[15] On-the-job training is the norm.

As a consequence, when crises do erupt, they are typically managed in a makeshift manner. Personnel are pulled from their regular assignments, responses are hastily prepared, and funds are hurriedly reprogrammed if they can be.[16] Perversely, this practice reinforces the conviction—arguably hubris—of many experienced policymakers that they have little new to learn about what to do in a crisis. What useful knowledge they accrue, moreover, dissipates as soon as they leave office. No effort is made to capture the best practices or management recommendations of senior officials and incorporate them into professional training and education courses for those who follow.

This failure to learn systematically from the past means that there is no established body of specialized knowledge to inform and guide policymakers on how to avert or manage foreign policy crises. Compared to the U.S. military's well-researched doctrine for executing specific missions at different levels of command, nothing remotely similar exists for directing and orchestrating civilian tools and capacities for crisis prevention and management.[17] This problem is especially egregious at the Department of State. As a recently retired deputy secretary of state admitted after more than thirty-five years serving in various capacities both in Washington and abroad: "There is no playbook or operating manual in the Foreign Service, and the absence of diplomatic doctrine, or even systematic case studies, has been a long-standing weakness of the State Department."[18]

OVERCOMING THE CHALLENGE

Shifting the attention of U.S. policymakers to managing potential threats, and not just the crisis of the day, cannot be achieved by simply exhorting them to do so. Nor will a few well-intentioned institutional reforms have much effect. A comprehensive systemic approach made up of the following interconnected and mutually supporting initiatives is required to reorient the United States and change behavior in a fundamental way.

Develop an Overarching Concept of Operations

U.S. policymakers need an overarching concept of operations that articulates how the goal of preventing and managing foreign policy crises can be accomplished using the resources available across the entire U.S. government. Without one, policymakers will continue to flounder and the resulting effort will always be less than the sum of its parts. This operational concept or theory of change has to be more than a crude policy framework that assigns roles and missions to departments with the hope that their representatives will figure out what to do and how to work together. Identifying all the instruments in the U.S. government toolbox will not help much, either—certainly not without a manual for how to use the instruments in defined circumstances.

The tried and trusted strategy used by public health professionals, and in public security and risk management, offers the most promising solution.[19] This multilayered approach progressively uses different preventive measures at different stages in the evolution of a specific problem or risk. It can be readily adapted to prevent and mitigate the most common sources of political instability and conflict that account for most of the United States' foreign policy crises. It would consist of three complementary areas of activity, as described in the 2009 report:

- *Conflict risk reduction.* These are measures taken to minimize potential sources of instability and conflict before they arise. They encompass efforts to reduce the impact of specific threats, such as controlling the development of destabilizing weapons systems or arms transfers that may cause regional power imbalances, restricting the influence of dangerous nonstate actors, and diminishing the possible harm from anticipated demographic, economic, and environmental change. At the same time, these measures promote conditions conducive to peace and stability. Within states, these measures include encouraging equitable economic development, good governance, rule of law, and respect for human rights. Stability can be enhanced through rules on the use of force, military and economic cooperation, security guarantees, confidence-building measures, functional integration, and effective arbitration mechanisms, among other things. Risk reduction measures, moreover, can be applied globally for systemic benefits or focused on a specific region or state.

- *Crisis prevention.* In regions or states that are particularly volatile or susceptible to violence, a similar set of measures can help prevent the situation from deteriorating further. Much like risk reduction efforts, crisis prevention measures can be aimed at redressing the specific sources or drivers of instability and potential conflict or assisting the states or groups that are threatened. A host of diplomatic, economic, legal, and military measures could alter either the contributing conditions or the decision calculus of the parties to the potential conflict. These include cooperative measures (such as diplomatic persuasion and mediation, economic assistance and incentives, legal arbitration, and military support) as well as coercive instruments (diplomatic condemnation and isolation, economic sanctions, legal action, preventive military deployments, and threats of punitive action). The two are not mutually exclusive and are frequently seen as most effective when applied together—as carrots and sticks.

- *Crisis mitigation.* If earlier preventive efforts fail to have the desired effect or if violence erupts with little to no warning, then many of the same basic techniques can be employed to manage and mitigate the crisis. These measures include efforts to facilitate cooperative dispute resolution and change incentive structures to promote peaceful outcomes. Thus, steps can be taken to identify and empower moderates, isolate or deter potential spoilers, and sway the uncommitted. More interventionist measures to protect endangered groups or secure sensitive areas through observer missions, arms embargoes (or arms supplies), and preventive military or police deployments are also conceivable. Moreover, in some circumstances, preventive initiatives could be equally helpful in containing a relatively localized crisis or flash point to help ensure that it does not spread or draw in others. In some other cases, containment could realistically be the only crisis mitigation option. The various measures have to be mixed and matched to the specific circumstances and guided by a similarly tailored political strategy.[20]

This overarching concept of operations can be applied to any crisis. Specific playbooks could be developed for commonly occurring contingencies such as territorial disputes, terrorist incidents, and weapons of mass destruction (WMD)–related crises, as well as potentially destabilizing instances of electoral violence or unconstitutional transfers of power such as coups d'état. Much the same approach can be used for crisis management when deliberate de-escalation strategies and techniques can be elaborated in advance. Playbooks have other benefits than simply bringing greater rigor and coherence to U.S. policymaking. By making it more likely that a range of options can be considered readily, they can speed up decision-making while helping to properly synchronize and coordinate complex operations.[21]

Augment Early Warning With Strategic Foresight

The early-warning systems that the United States uses to alert senior officials of threatening developments are important and necessary. But these systems are essentially reactive in that the alarm is sounded—at least in a way likely to be heard—only when there is compelling evidence of a threat. This arrangement decreases the time and potential opportunities to implement preventive and/or precautionary measures, which can be further limited by well-known cognitive and organizational problems that impede timely warning, such as mirror imaging and groupthink biases.[22] However, by anticipating threats—before they materialize and become more menacing—warning systems can address the sources of potential concern sooner and in potentially more cost-effective ways.

That is the theory at least. In practice, anticipating potentially threatening developments in a way that is helpful to policymakers is, in some respects, even more daunting. Scanning the horizon for things to worry about opens up countless possibilities that could just as easily paralyze early action as motivate it. Moreover, analysts and policymakers face the question of how far into the future they should look. Too far and policymakers are likely to dismiss a potential source of concern as something that could just as easily improve as it could worsen. Even if the concern appeared warranted, the policymaker might not be incentivized to act if the concern seems unlikely to materialize within a foreseeable time frame.

Anticipation is achievable, however, through disciplined strategic foresight. Knowing what kinds of events have triggered a crisis for the United States in the past is helpful for anticipating what similar circumstances might arise and have the same effect in the future. As the U.S. foreign policy crises since the end of the Cold War reveal, precipitating events have a recurring character (see the list of U.S. foreign policy crises from 1989 to 2019, pages 18–23 in this report). Although the context and actors may have differed, each crisis was triggered by an event or series of events that either directly threatened the United States or its allies, challenged or violated a cardinal norm of international behavior, increased the risk of WMD proliferation or use, had the potential to seriously destabilize a region, or undermined peace and stability in a country, with potentially severe humanitarian consequences. Knowing the risk factors and other warning indicators associated with the onset of such events allows for at least an initial assessment of what might be plausible in specific places and at certain times in the future. More in-depth analysis can corroborate or invalidate the initial assessment.

Foresight exercises of this kind can be carried out for different time horizons, but logically they should be calibrated to the usual lead time required for the implementation of measures to prevent or mitigate a specific concern. Twelve to eighteen months could be considered a good time frame for crisis prevention purposes. It is close enough to convince busy policymakers about the plausibility of specific concerns but not so close as to preclude meaningful preventive or precautionary action.

Using a foresight technique that combines estimates of both the likelihood and potential impact of events on U.S. interests—what a classic risk assessment should do—allows policymakers to focus on the most threatening sources of concern. Policy priorities can in turn be set in a truly strategic and defensible way.

For the last ten years, the Center for Preventive Action has conducted an annual Preventive Priorities Survey (PPS) of U.S. foreign policy experts using this basic risk assessment approach. Toward the end of each calendar year, a public crowdsourcing process generates a list of plausible crisis contingencies for the coming twelve months. Of these contingencies, the top thirty are chosen for a survey that asks respondents to evaluate both the likelihood and potential impact on U.S. interests of each contingency according to defined criteria. The scores for each contingency are then aggregated and sorted into three tiers of relative policy priority using a standard risk matrix. The criteria and prioritization methodology can be seen in figure 1.

Although the PPS is a relatively crude foresight exercise, the results have more than demonstrated the value of such horizon scanning, particularly for generating consensus about the relative priority of specific concerns. For example, the PPS for 2019 identified Venezuela's deepening economic and political crisis and the possibility of armed conflict between the United States and Iran as top tier priorities—both of which have, in fact, become serious concerns. An exercise similar to the PPS should be adopted and complemented by other foresight techniques.[23]

Institutionalize Policy Planning and Preparedness

Strategic foresight is only useful, of course, if it triggers timely policy planning and, ultimately, the implementation of specific preventive and precautionary measures. Such preparations are only likely to take place if they are properly institutionalized and routinized. One way to do this is by legally mandating policy planning, just as the Department of Defense is required to plan for military contingencies.[24] Another is to establish a formal triggering mechanism linked to the strategic foresight process discussed above so that identified concerns that match specified criteria are referred automatically for policy planning.

This latter approach is currently used by CPA for its own contingency planning exercises. Most, if not all, of the thirty-five Contingency Planning Memoranda (CPMs) that have been commissioned to study potential sources of instability or conflict over the last ten years had originally been identified in the annual PPS. Many proved to be prescient of later events, as illustrated by the following excerpts:

- "Crisis Between Ukraine and Russia," July 2009: Steven Pifer warned of the growing risk of a major confrontation between Russia and Ukraine in Crimea. He argued that since U.S. tools to manage a crisis

Figure 1. PREVENTIVE PRIORITIES SURVEY 2020
RISK MATRIX AND DEFINITIONS

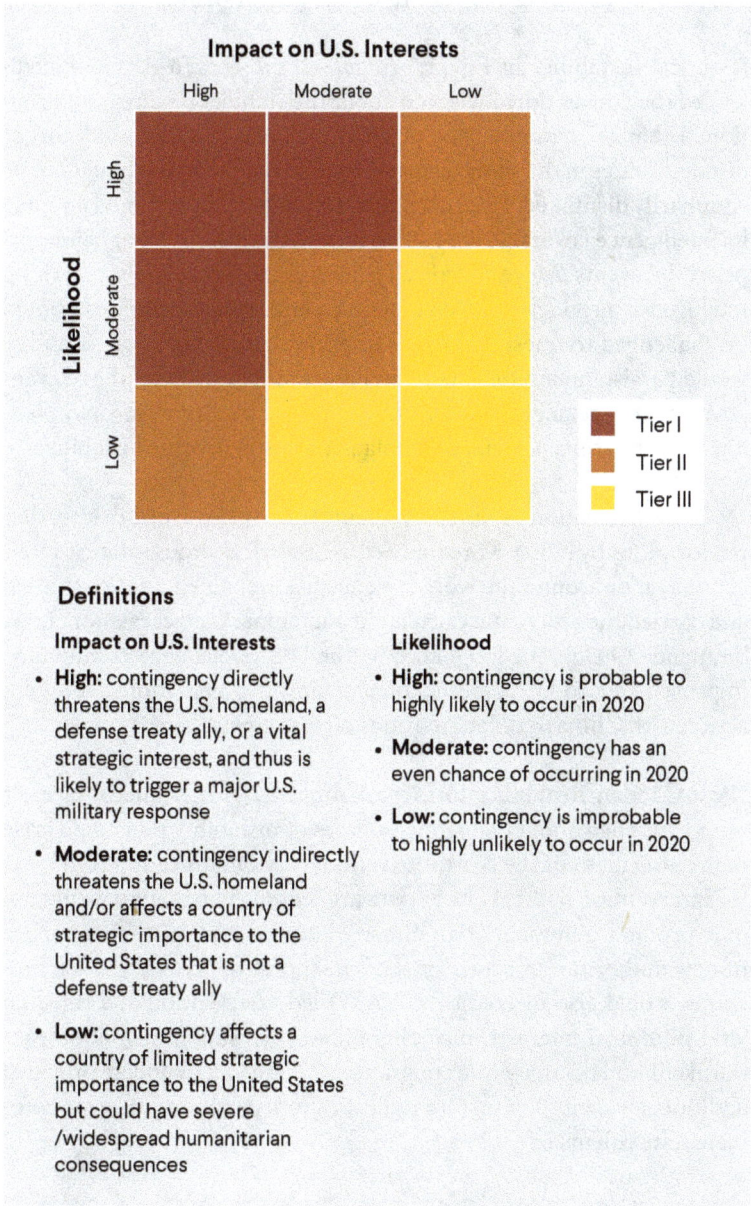

Impact on U.S. Interests

	High	Moderate	Low

Likelihood

High	Tier I	Tier I	Tier II
Moderate	Tier I	Tier II	Tier III
Low	Tier II	Tier III	Tier III

Legend:
- ■ Tier I
- ■ Tier II
- ■ Tier III

Definitions

Impact on U.S. Interests

- **High:** contingency directly threatens the U.S. homeland, a defense treaty ally, or a vital strategic interest, and thus is likely to trigger a major U.S. military response

- **Moderate:** contingency indirectly threatens the U.S. homeland and/or affects a country of strategic importance to the United States that is not a defense treaty ally

- **Low:** contingency affects a country of limited strategic importance to the United States but could have severe /widespread humanitarian consequences

Likelihood

- **High:** contingency is probable to highly likely to occur in 2020

- **Moderate:** contingency has an even chance of occurring in 2020

- **Low:** contingency is improbable to highly unlikely to occur in 2020

Source: Paul B. Stares, *Preventive Priorities Survey 2020* (New York: Council on Foreign Relations, 2019).

were limited, greater effort should be placed on preventing a crisis from breaking out. To do this, he proposed strengthening links between the West and Ukraine before a possible crisis, which could help discourage Russia from initiating a conflict or overplaying its hand.[25]

- "Political Instability in Egypt," August 2009: Steven A. Cook challenged the conventional wisdom about the stability of Egypt and cautioned that the potential for growing political volatility and abrupt discontinuities in the short term (six to eighteen months) should not be summarily dismissed. He argued that the United States should upgrade its intelligence coverage of Egypt to reduce the likelihood of being surprised by events. More specifically, he suggested that analysts writing intelligence products and conducting contingency exercises should be challenged to question the assumption that authoritarian stability would persist indefinitely in Egypt. He also suggested that the relevant government agencies and departments should begin contingency planning around scenarios that could plausibly result in acute instability.[26]

- "Military Escalation in Korea," November 2010: I warned that further provocations by North Korea, as well as other dangerous military interactions on or around the Korean Peninsula, remained a serious threat and carried the risk of miscalculation and unintended escalation. I recommended heightened vigilance by the U.S intelligence community, improvements to U.S.-South Korea defensive preparations, and joint action with China to reduce tensions on the peninsula.[27]

- "Post-Qaddafi Instability in Libya," August 2011: Daniel P. Serwer bluntly warned about dangerous sources of instability that could arise in the aftermath of the North Atlantic Treaty Organization (NATO)–led intervention in 2011. As Serwer argued, such instability would not only produce a humanitarian disaster but also lead to the emergence of new authoritarian leader or the breakup of the country. Such outcomes would also discredit the NATO-led intervention and threaten vital European interests, including oil and gas supplies, and increase the likelihood of large-scale emigration.[28] A June 2015 update provided additional warnings of further radicalization, partition, and even complete state collapse.[29]

- "Armed Clash in the South China Sea," April 2012: Bonnie S. Glaser assessed that although the possibility of a major military conflict in the South China Sea was low, the potential for a violent clash in the near future was high. Accordingly, Glaser set out a collection of initiatives to build trust, prevent conflict, and avoid escalation.[30] In a 2015 update, she warned of China's construction of artificial islands and assessed that these islands would enable China to extend the range of its navy, air force, coast guard, and fishing fleets in just a few years.[31]

- "Political Unrest in Venezuela," September 2012: Patrick Duddy argued that Venezuela could experience significant political unrest and violence, leading to the further curtailment of democracy.[32] In a March 2015 update, he provided additional analysis of the worsening economic and social situation inside Venezuela.[33]

- "Armed Confrontation Between India and China," November 2015: Daniel S. Markey highlighted the growing potential for a dangerous crisis between China and India, particularly should a border clash in a disputed area take place. Given the risk that a serious crisis would pose for the United States, the report laid out a host of preventive and remedial measures.[34]

- "Strategic Reversal in Afghanistan," June 2016: Seth G. Jones warned of both a Taliban resurgence and a fragile Afghan government for U.S. efforts in Afghanistan. Given the significant level of U.S. engagement, he recommended that U.S. policy focus on resolving acute political challenges within the Afghan government—and with the Taliban—while also maintaining support for U.S. and Afghan forces.[35]

Contingency planning rarely anticipates precisely how and when events play out, but that does not invalidate its utility. Policymakers can still hedge against the general risk of a specific contingency in useful ways. Many crisis response options, moreover, remain relevant regardless of what may transpire.[36] Discussing these options in advance—their risks and their implementation requirements—is clearly preferable to doing so under pressure and time constraints.

Such planning should be done in a way that policymakers find useful and, crucially, in a way that motivates them to take preventive or precautionary measures. Here again, CPA's experience with its contingency planning reports offers some useful pointers. Each CPM follows a prescribed format, beginning with a clear assessment of the specific contingency—or variations thereof—including how it could be triggered and how it could plausibly evolve. The principal parties involved in the contingency are identified, along with any information that sheds light on their motives, means, or opportunities to act in the way prescribed. Recognizing who the central actors are is critical to developing specific policy measures that could influence behavior both before and during a crisis. Warning indicators associated with the contingency are also identified. These indicators prepare officials to recognize specific danger signs and set markers for potential policy responses.

Because policymakers may not be fully cognizant of the implications of the contingency, each CPM also assesses how the contingency could threaten U.S. interests and thus why taking preventive or precautionary measures is desirable, if not essential. The goal is to avoid generalized statements or discuss only first-order effects. The assessment conveys what is at stake—both the immediate and proximate consequences—as well as any wider and long-term ripple effects on U.S. interests. The latter are clearly conditional, but the possibilities can often be bounded in helpful ways.

Such assessments provide the necessary foundation for the policy analysis component of the CPMs. Individual sections are reserved for the discussion of preventive and mitigating policy options—the former are designed to lessen the likelihood of the contingency and the latter its potential harm should it materialize. The goal is to explore in a reasonable and balanced way the full range of relevant options from the menu of measures outlined earlier and to do so as rigorously as possible so that each option is evaluated according to common criteria—potential costs, risks, feasibility, and likelihood of success. On the basis of this assessment, a package of recommendations is presented.

Just as identifying commonly recurring types of crises can help with anticipation, categorizing by contingency type can also help with planning. This approach can be readily adapted to consider different types of crises, whether they are caused by threats to the U.S. homeland, the proliferation of weapons of mass destruction, the risk of regional military escalation from localized disputes, or internal political instability. Different preventive strategies and policy tools—in essence, tailored playbooks—can be developed for the most common types of contingencies that have triggered foreign policy crises in the past. CPA's work in this area again demonstrates how this can be accomplished.

Five CPMs representing different types of contingencies have been included in the appendix to illustrate this point. Robert K. Knake's "A Cyberattack on the U.S. Power Grid" examines a growing homeland security concern; Steven Simon's "An Israeli Strike on Iran" discusses the escalatory risks associated with counter-proliferation operations; and Michael S. Chase's "Averting a Cross-Strait Crisis" looks at how the United States can help prevent and manage a contingency involving both an ally and another major power. George F. Ward's "Political Instability in Zimbabwe" and Shannon K. O'Neil's "A Venezuelan Refugee Crisis" both focus on the humanitarian and regional spillover risks of domestic political instability.

These exemplar CPMs illustrate what can be accomplished with modest resources. Clearly, the United States, with all its analytical and policy planning resources, can do much more.

CONCLUSION AND RECOMMENDATIONS

The United States should devote more attention and resources to being better prepared to avert and manage future foreign policy crises. In all likelihood, the world will grow more turbulent in the coming years and the number of occasions when the president is confronted with difficult choices will increase. The stakes in any future crisis are also likely to be greater—whether it is because another major power is involved or due to the growing systemic risks of a highly interconnected world. In short, the margins for error are narrowing and the potential costs for the United States, including its long-term standing in the world, are growing.

Implementing the aforementioned proposals to make the United States more forward-looking and forward-acting would not be inherently difficult or disruptive. Nor would these suggestions require substantial resources. However, political will and a clear declaration of intent from the president and other senior officials that crisis prevention and management is an institutional and programmatic priority of the United States are required. Without a high-level demand signal from the White House, any effort to make the United States more anticipatory and proactive will likely fizzle. The opportunity to do this, moreover, will be greatest at the start of a new administration or four-year term. More specifically, the United States should do the following:

- *Prioritize the importance of crisis prevention and mitigation in official speeches and other declarations, particularly in the U.S. national security strategy and associated internal policy directives.* The overarching approach should be to promote policies known to lower the general risk of conflict and instability over the long term, anticipate potential crises that pose the greatest risk involving the U.S. military in the medium term so that deliberate preventive initiatives can be prioritized and implemented, and enhance U.S. preparedness to respond rapidly and effectively to crises that arise in the short term.

- *Institute a regular, government-wide strategic foresight and risk assessment process to anticipate and prioritize potential sources of instability and conflict that could threaten U.S. interests and trigger future crises.* This should begin with a baseline assessment at the beginning of each administration that would provide the foundation for an integrated national security watch list or risk matrix to be reviewed and updated every six months. The Office of the Director of National Intelligence should maintain this product according to parameters and priorities set by the National Security Council (NSC). As such, this new foresight effort should build on recent initiatives to reconstitute a regular and more forward-looking warning process within the U.S. intelligence community, particularly since the national warning staff at the National Intelligence Council was disbanded in 2008.[37]

- *Establish a regular interagency policy planning process focused on a prioritized set of risks or contingencies identified in the strategic foresight exercise.* The NSC should lead and coordinate these parallel but connected processes: one would focus on the design and coordination of policies aimed at reducing the likelihood of a specific contingency and the other on managing the contingency should it materialize. Contingency planning of this kind has been done well in the past but requires a dedicated institutional mechanism with high-level backing to ensure that the work outsourced to the relevant agencies is given requisite priority.

- *Improve the readiness of the NSC and other senior officials to manage serious national security crises.* This should ensure not only that officials are appropriately trained and knowledgeable of standing procedures but also that they regularly participate in realistic exercises.[38] The ability to stand up crisis response teams rapidly, and with the capacity to review extant plans or generate new ones as needed, is critical. Generic playbooks and checklists could also be developed in advance to support decision-making under pressured conditions. New decision-support aids to help policymakers in moments of deep uncertainty should also be explored, including data-driven approaches that use algorithms, artificial intelligence, or machine learning to assess risk (so-called decision intelligence).

- *Enhance the standard of professional training for diplomats and other officials to manage commonly occurring contingencies.* This training should draw on a deliberate effort to capture best practices and lessons learned from prior experience so that they can be incorporated into future training.[39]

These initiatives will not preclude the United States from being surprised by and unprepared for future crises. But they will certainly reduce the chances of this happening and thus lower the likelihood that future presidents will regret that they had not done more to avert a particular crisis or manage it better.

U.S. FOREIGN POLICY CRISES, 1989–2019

The Center for Preventive Action (CPA) at the Council on Foreign Relations compiled the following list of U.S. foreign policy crises since the end of the Cold War (November 1989) according to these criteria:

- The triggering event or series of events is perceived as a threat to U.S. interests or values such that it may warrant the use of U.S. armed forces to protect them.

- The perception of threat is sufficient to attract high level U.S. government attention (deputies level and above) principally, but not exclusively, in the executive branch.

- Decision-making is driven by a strong sense of urgency based on the belief that there is a finite or optimal time frame to respond. It can also be accompanied by considerable uncertainty about the nature of the threatening event(s) and what action to take in response, owing to doubts about efficacy and cost.

An initial list of crises was produced using datasets generated by Duke University's International Crisis Behavior project, the Correlates of War project, and the U.S. government-sponsored Political Instability Task Force, as well as conflict background briefs and lists from the Congressional Research Service and RAND Corporation that tabulate cases of U.S. military deployments since the Cold War.[1] Additional sources were also consulted, including U.S. government press releases and other communiques, as well as the memoirs of presidents and senior government officials. This list runs to the beginning of October 2019, but because CPA relied on publicly available press releases and unclassified reports to determine whether an event merited inclusion in its list of crises, the final list may not include recent or still classified events.

The final list clearly reflects CPA's judgment about which crises to include or exclude. In particular, CPA included certain humanitarian crises and natural disasters for which the deployment of U.S. military personnel was deemed important to securing U.S. interests. However, CPA did not include crises that were precipitated by economic events, even though they might have had an international dimension; in almost all such cases, the use of military force was irrelevant or uncalled for. CPA also excluded many terrorist attacks and related incidents involving U.S. forces as well as U.S. allies and partners, assessing that these events were part of the global war on terror following the September 11, 2001, attacks on the United States. These events are already covered comprehensively in other databases.[2]

Deciding whether some events are discrete enough to warrant being listed individually or should be classified as part of a single, prolonged crisis, is also a subjective call. For example, some experts could justifiably argue that the various events related to the Balkans in the 1990s constituted one long crisis. The same rationale applies to episodic events related to North Korea's development of nuclear weapons and long-range missiles and for the ongoing conflict in Syria. For some crises, CPA chose to distinguish between different events of the same provenance because they triggered an urgent reassessment of U.S. policy and thus justified treatment as separate crises. In addition, for crises that could be linked to multiyear events, such as the European refugee crisis, CPA selected the year of the crisis based on when it triggered the most urgent alarm in the U.S. government.

Figure 2. U.S. FOREIGN POLICY CRISES, 1989–2019

George H.W. Bush

1989	Attempted coup in the Philippines against Corazon Aquino
	U.S. invasion of Panama
1990	India-Pakistan nuclear crisis
	First Liberian Civil War
	Iraq's invasion and occupation of Kuwait
1991	Bosnian and Croat independence movements
	Uprisings in northern and southern Iraq
	Breakup of Yugoslavia
	Attempted coup against Mikhail Gorbachev
	Coup in Haiti
1992	Coup in Sierra Leone
	Coup and famine in Somalia

Bill Clinton

1993	Terrorist bombing attack on World Trade Center in New York
	Assassination attempt on George H.W. Bush in Kuwait
	Russian constitutional crisis
	First Battle of Mogadishu, Somalia
	Coup in Burundi
1994	Siege of Sarajevo
	Rwandan genocide
	North Korean nuclear crisis
	Iraqi threats to Kuwait
	Chechnya secession and First Chechen War
1995	Attack on UN safe haven in Srebrenica and Srebrenica massacre
	China-Taiwan crisis
1996	Unrest in Liberia
	Israeli military intervention in Lebanon
	Armed mutinies in Central African Republic
	Khobar Towers bombing in Saudi Arabia
	Iraqi offensive in Kurdistan
	North Korean submarine infiltration

Bill Clinton (cont.)

1997   Rebellion in Albania

        Civil war in Sierra Leone

        Coup in Cambodia

        Armed conflict in Congo-Brazzaville

1998   Serbian invasion of Kosovo

        Eritrea-Ethiopia border war

        India and Pakistan nuclear tests

        Second Congo War

        U.S. embassy bombings in Kenya and Tanzania

        North Korean missile test over Sea of Japan

        Violent unrest in Liberia

        Hurricane Mitch in Central America

1999   Atrocities in Kosovo

        India-Pakistan conflict in Kargil

        Second Chechen War

        Independence of East Timor

        Flash floods in northern Venezuela

2000   Ethiopian offensive against Eritrea

        Bombing of the USS *Cole*

George W. Bush

2001   Hainan Island incident in the South China Sea

        9/11 attacks

        Twin Peaks crisis between India and Pakistan

2002   Insurgency in southern Philippines

        Military unrest in Ivory Coast

2003   Genocide in Darfur, Sudan

        Alleged Iraqi violations of weapons of mass destruction prohibitions

        Second Liberian civil war

2004   Coup in Haiti

        Indian Ocean tsunami

2005   Earthquake in Kashmir

George W. Bush (cont.)

2006   Iranian nuclear enrichment

Second Lebanese War

First North Korean nuclear test

2007   Construction of Syrian nuclear reactor

Electoral violence in Kenya

2008   Sri Lankan Civil War

Russia–Georgia War

Conflict in Gaza

Barack Obama

2009   North Korean nuclear test

Al-Qaeda in the Arabian Peninsula threats in Yemen

2010   Earthquake in Haiti

Sinking of the South Korean naval ship *Cheonan*

Second Kyrgyz Revolution

Flooding in Pakistan

Bombardment of Yeonpyeong Island in the South China Sea

2011   Violent unrest in Egypt

Post-election violence in Ivory Coast

Threat of mass atrocities in Libya

Fukushima Daiichi nuclear disaster in Japan

Violent crackdown in Syria

2012   Coup in Mali

Scarborough Shoal standoff in the South China Sea

Attack on U.S. embassy in Benghazi, Libya

Conflict in Gaza

Seizure of Goma, Democratic Republic of Congo

2013   North Korean nuclear test

Mass atrocities in Central African Republic

Chemical weapons attack in Damascus, Syria

Civil war in South Sudan

2014   Russia-Ukraine conflict

Boko Haram attacks in northern Nigeria

Islamic State operations in Iraq and Syria

Barack Obama (cont.)

2014   Conflict in Gaza

Ebola outbreak in Guinea, Liberia, and Sierra Leone

Islamic State mass atrocities against Yazidis

2015   Boko Haram attacks in Cameroon

Saudi-led military intervention in Yemen

Violent unrest in Burundi

European refugee crisis

Russian intervention in Syrian civil war

2016   North Korean nuclear test

Russian interference in U.S. presidential elections

Violent clashes in Juba, South Sudan

Coup attempt in Turkey

North Korean nuclear test

Missile attacks against USS *Mason*

Donald J. Trump

2017   Chemical weapons attack in Khan Shaykhun, Syria

WannaCry ransomware attack

Islamic State seizure of Marawi, Philippines

Saudi-led blockade of Qatar

North Korean intercontinental ballistic missile test

Mass atrocities in Rakhine State, Myanmar

North Korean nuclear test

Ambush of U.S. soldiers in Niger

2018   Turkish offensive in Afrin, Syria

Chemical weapons attack in Douma, Syria

2019   Political and social unrest in Venezuela

India-Pakistan border skirmishes

Violent unrest in Sudan

U.S. confrontation with Iran

APPENDIX:
SELECT CONTINGENCY
PLANNING MEMORANDA

A CYBERATTACK ON THE U.S. POWER GRID

Robert K. Knake

The U.S. power grid has long been considered a logical target for a major cyberattack. Besides the intrinsic importance of the power grid to a functioning U.S. society, all sixteen sectors of the U.S. economy deemed to make up the nation's critical infrastructure rely on electricity. Disabling or otherwise interfering with the power grid in a significant way could thus seriously harm the United States.

Carrying out a cyberattack that successfully disrupts grid operations would be extremely difficult but not impossible. Such an attack would require months of planning, significant resources, and a team with a broad range of expertise. Although cyberattacks by terrorist and criminal organizations cannot be ruled out, the capabilities necessary to mount a major operation against the U.S. power grid make potential state adversaries the principal threat.

Attacks on power grids are no longer a theoretical concern. In 2015, an attacker took down parts of a power grid in Ukraine. Although attribution was not definitive, geopolitical circumstances and forensic evidence suggest Russian involvement. A year later, Russian hackers targeted a transmission level substation, blacking out part of Kiev. In 2014, Admiral Michael Rogers, director of the National Security Agency, testified before the U.S. Congress that China and a few other countries likely had the capability to shut down the U.S. power grid. Iran, as an emergent cyber actor, could acquire such capability. Rapid digitization combined with low levels of investment in cybersecurity and a weak regulatory

---

This Contingency Planning Memorandum was originally published in April 2017. See Robert K. Knake, "A Cyberattack on the U.S. Power Grid," Council on Foreign Relations, April 2017, http://cfr.org/report/cyberattack-us-power-grid.

regime suggest that the U.S. power system is as vulnerable—if not more vulnerable—to a cyberattack as systems in other parts of the world.

An adversary with the capability to exploit vulnerabilities within the U.S. power grid might be motivated to carry out such an attack under a variety of circumstances. An attack on the power grid could be part of a coordinated military action, intended as a signaling mechanism during a crisis, or as a punitive measure in response to U.S. actions in some other arena. In each case, the United States should consider not only the potential damage and disruption caused by a cyberattack but also its broader effects on U.S. actions at the time it occurs. With respect to the former, a cyberattack could cause power losses in large portions of the United States that could last days in most places and up to several weeks in others. The economic costs would be substantial. As for the latter concern, the U.S. response or non-response could harm U.S. interests. Thus, the United States should take measures to prevent a cyberattack on its power grid and mitigate the potential harm should preventive efforts fail.

CONTINGENCY

The U.S. power system has evolved into a highly complex enterprise: 3,300 utilities that work together to deliver power through 200,000 miles of high-voltage transmission lines; 55,000 substations; and 5.5 million miles of distribution lines that bring power to millions of homes and businesses. Any of the system's principal elements—power generation, transmission, or distribution—could be targeted for a cyberattack. In the Ukraine case, attackers targeted substations that lower transmission voltages for distribution to consumers. Lloyd's of London, an insurance underwriter, developed a plausible scenario for an attack on the Eastern Interconnection—one of the two major electrical grids in the continental United States—which services roughly half the country. The hypothetical attack targeted power generators to cause a blackout covering fifteen states and the District of Columbia, leaving ninety-three million people without power. Other experts have concluded that an attack on the system for transmitting power from generation to end consumers would have devastating consequences. In one scenario, disruption of just nine transformers could cause widespread outages. Many experts are now also concerned that smart grid technologies, which use the internet to connect to power meters and appliances, could allow an attacker to take over thousands—if not millions—of unprotected devices, preventing power from being delivered to end users.

Regardless of which part of the power grid is targeted, attackers would need to conduct extensive research, gain initial access to utility business networks (likely through spearphishing), work to move through the business networks to gain access to control systems, and then identify targeted systems and develop the capability to disable them. Such sophisticated actions would require extensive planning by an organization able to recruit and coordinate a team that has a broad set of capabilities and is willing to devote many months, if not years, to the effort. State actors, therefore, are the more likely perpetrators, and given these long lead times, U.S. adversaries have likely already begun this process in anticipation of conflict. It is doubtful that a terrorist organization would have both the intent and means to carry out such an attack successfully. In the future, however, criminal groups could pose a real threat. They are growing in sophistication and in some cases rival, if not exceed, the capabilities of nation states. Payments for ransomware—malicious software that encrypts data and will not provide a code to unlock it unless a ransom has been paid—by some estimates have topped $300 million. This funding could allow criminal groups to purchase more sophisticated capabilities to carry out the ultimate ransomware attack.

The likelihood that an attack carried out by a determined and capable adversary would be thwarted by security measures is low. While some U.S. utilities might block attempts by an adversary to gain initial access or might be able to detect an adversary in their systems, many might not have the necessary tools in place to detect and respond. Efforts to improve data sharing that could enable detection by one company to block access across the entire industry are in their infancy. In the Lloyd's scenario, only 10 percent of targeted generators needed to be taken down to cause a widespread blackout.

Short of outright conflict with a state adversary, several plausible scenarios in which the U.S. power grid would be subject to cyberattack need to be considered:

- *Discrediting operations.* Given the importance of electricity to the daily lives of Americans, an adversary may see advantage in disrupting service to undermine public support for a U.S. administration at a politically sensitive time.

- *Distracting operations.* A state contemplating a diplomatic or military initiative likely to be opposed by the United States could carry out a cyberattack against the U.S. power grid that would distract the attention of the U.S. government and disrupt or delay its response.

- *Retaliatory operations.* In response to U.S. actions considered threatening by another state, such as the imposition of economic sanctions and various forms of political warfare, a cyberattack on the power grid could be carried out to punish the United States or intimidate it from taking further action with the implied threat of further damage.

There are many plausible circumstances in which states that possess the capability to conduct cyberattacks on the U.S. power grid—principally Russia and China, and potentially Iran and North Korea—could contemplate such action for the reasons elaborated above. However, considerable potential exists to miscalculate both the impact of a cyberattack on the U.S. grid and how the U.S. government might respond. Attacks could easily inflict much greater damage than intended, in good part because the many health and safety systems that depend on electricity could fail as well, resulting in widespread injuries and fatalities. Given the fragility of many industrial control systems, even reconnaissance activity risks accidentally causing harm. An adversary could also underestimate the ability of the United States to attribute the source of a cyberattack, with important implications for what happens thereafter. Thus, an adversary's expectations that it could attack the power grid anonymously and with impunity could be unfounded.

WARNING INDICATORS

A series of warning indicators would likely foretell a cyberattack on the U.S. power grid. Potential indicators could include smaller test-run attacks outside the United States on systems that are used in the United

States; intelligence collection that indicates an adversary is conducting reconnaissance or is in the planning stages; deterioration in relations leading to escalatory steps such as increased intelligence operations, hostile rhetoric, and recurring threats; and increased probing of electric sector networks and/or the implementation of malware that is detected by more sophisticated utilities.

IMPLICATIONS FOR U.S. INTERESTS

A large-scale cyberattack on the U.S. power grid could inflict considerable damage. The 2003 Northeast Blackout left fifty million people without power for four days and caused economic losses between $4 billion and $10 billion. The Lloyd's scenario estimates economic costs of $243 billion and a small rise in death rates as health and safety systems fail. While darker scenarios envision scarcity of water and food, deterioration of sanitation, and a breakdown in security, leading to a societal collapse, it would be possible to mitigate the worst effects of the outage and have power restored to most areas within days. At this level of damage, the American public would likely demand a forceful response, which could reshape U.S. geopolitical interests for decades. Traditional military action, as opposed to a response in kind, would be likely.

In addition to the direct consequences of a cyberattack, how the United States responds also has implications for its management of the situation that may have prompted the attack in the first place, the state of relations with the apparent perpetrator, the perceived vulnerability of the United States, and the evolution of international norms on cyberwarfare.

How the U.S. government reacts, more than the actual harm done, will determine whether the cyberattack has a continuing impact on geopolitics. If the incident reveals a U.S. vulnerability in cyberspace that can be targeted to deter the United States from taking action abroad, the implications of the incident would be profound. If, on the other hand, the U.S. government shows firm resolve in the face of the attack and does not change its behavior in the interest of the attacker, the event is unlikely to have significant consequences for the role of the United States abroad.

On the domestic front, a highly disruptive attack would likely upend the model of private sector responsibility for cybersecurity. As was done with aviation security after 9/11, Congress would likely move quickly to take over responsibility for protecting the grid from cyberattack by either creating a new agency or granting new authorities to an existing agency such as U.S. Cyber Command. Such a move would likely reduce the efficiency of grid operations and open the door to expanding government's role in protecting other sectors of the economy. A devastating attack might also prompt calls to create a national firewall, like China and other countries have, to inspect all traffic at national borders. However, the experience of other countries and the technical reality of the internet suggest that these firewalls are ineffective for cybersecurity but well suited to restricting speech online and censoring information.

PREVENTIVE OPTIONS

Preventing an attack will require improving the security of the power grid as well as creating a deterrence posture that would dissuade adversaries from attacking it. The goal of such a strategy should be to secure the power grid to make it defensible, to detect attempts to compromise the security of the grid, and to provide certainty to adversaries that the United States will be able to attribute the attack and respond accordingly.

Protective Measures

Unlike enterprise information technology, the industrial control systems that control the power grid typically perform single functions and need to communicate only with a small set of other devices in routine patterns. Thus, securing these systems and detecting malicious activity should, in theory, be relatively simple. In practice, many industrial control systems are built on general computing systems from a generation ago. They were not designed with security in mind and cannot be updated. This problem has not been corrected with the latest generation of smart grid technologies; the Government Accountability Office (GAO) has found that these devices often lack the ability to authenticate administrators and cannot maintain activity logs necessary for forensic analysis, among other deficiencies. These devices are often accessible from the public internet and use weak authentication mechanisms. Thus, improving the protection of the grid requires investing in new, more secure technology that can be protected and to implement basic cybersecurity hygiene. The challenge is, therefore, not to develop technical specifications to secure the grid but how to incentivize investment.

A regulatory approach could theoretically set a minimum standard, thereby leveling costs across all companies and addressing cost-cutting in security measures. Such a regimen—the Critical Infrastructure

Protection Standards established by the North America Electric Reliability Council (NERC)—has been in place for over a decade, though GAO has found that many standards remain voluntary and the extent to which utilities have implemented these standards is unknown. Raising and enforcing standards could help prevent a catastrophic attack by encouraging utilities to proactively defend their networks. A model for such an approach could be borrowed from the nuclear sector, where the Nuclear Regulatory Council has established so-called Design Basis Threats and requires nuclear plant operators to prove that they have the controls in place to defeat such threats. Yet, given the thin margins on which utilities operate, such an unfunded mandate is not likely to meaningfully improve security. Moreover, current federal requirements do not extend to power distribution, which is regulated unevenly at the state level.

As regulated entities with fees set by control boards, utilities do not have sufficient budgets to significantly increase security funding. Risk managers at utilities will argue that they must balance the possibility of a cyberattack against the near certainty that weather events will affect their customers. A decision to increase spending on cybersecurity could come at the expense of burying power lines, raising them above the tree line, or trimming trees along the lines. In 2016, the Department of Energy (DOE) received only three reports of cyber incidents at utilities; none of the incidents affected customers. In the same time period, forty-one weather events caused outages, affecting 5.2 million customers. Numbers for 2015 show a similar pattern. Thus, some form of rate relief is needed to encourage significant investments in cybersecurity.

More could also be done to improve government support for securing electric utilities. The DOE has run a pilot program, known as the Cybersecurity Risk Information Sharing Program (CRISP), for several years to help companies detect advanced threats targeting their networks. DOE labs have also funded research projects on the specific cybersecurity needs of utilities. Yet critics of the program argue that it is too expensive for most utilities to participate in and that it is only focused on detecting threats at network boundaries rather than within ICS networks. Expansion of intelligence and data sharing between the government and private companies, and among private companies themselves, could greatly reduce the chances of an attacker being capable of taking down multiple targets and causing a cascading effect. The Electricity Information Sharing and Analysis Center (E-ISAC) is mostly focused on physical threats and weather events. GAO found cybersecurity information sharing weak across the sector. Sectors such as finance and the defense industrial base have developed strong information sharing practices with government support. Emulating these efforts in the electricity sector would be a valuable government contribution to help owners and operators in the industry protect themselves.

Given the large number of utilities and the vast infrastructure to protect, even with improved cybersecurity, an adversary would still be likely to find numerous unprotected systems that can be disrupted. As the Lloyd's analysis concluded, only 10 percent of targeted generators needed to be taken offline to cause widespread harm. Therefore, improving the security of individual utilities alone is unlikely to significantly deter attackers. By focusing on detecting early signs of an attack and sharing that information within the sector and with the government, even when individual utilities fail to detect attacks on themselves, they can warn the government and other companies and help prevent wider disruption.

Deterrent Measures

Adversaries may underestimate both the ability of the U.S. government to determine who carried out an attack and the seriousness with which such an attack would be addressed. Law enforcement agencies such as the Federal Bureau of Investigation (FBI) and the U.S. Secret Service have built strong forensic investigation capabilities and strong relationships with both foreign law enforcement and the intelligence community. Through cooperation, the U.S. government has been able to determine the parties behind most major attacks. The Barack Obama administration publicly named the foreign actors behind some attacks and provided supporting evidence on a case-by-case basis. Making public attribution of attacks a routine practice could be a deterrent.

Beyond simply naming the adversary behind attacks, the U.S. government could make clear how it would view an attack on the power grid and the kinds of responses it would consider. Characterizing an attack on the power grid as an armed attack would likely have the strongest deterrent effect. Doing so would reflect the developing norms against peacetime attacks on critical infrastructure as agreed to in the UN Group of Governmental Experts. In keeping with these norms, the U.S. government could outline response options that would be proportional but not necessarily in kind. These response options would clarify how the U.S. government would respond not only to a successful attack but also to a failed attempt and to the discovery of adversarial probing and exploration to prepare for an attack.

In developing its policy, the U.S. government should keep in mind that a strong policy against targeting U.S. systems could constrain U.S. military options to target foreign systems. Yet, given the long lead times for carrying out a successful cyberattack campaign, labeling reconnaissance activities as hostile actions and limiting such activities by U.S. cyber operators could mean forgoing the ability to make significant use of cyber operations during a conflict.

MITIGATING OPTIONS

If an attack on the grid cannot be prevented, steps can be taken now to mitigate the effects of the attack and plan the response.

Pre-attack Measures

Actions taken now could significantly mitigate the effects of a large-scale blackout caused by a cyberattack. Maintaining and exercising manual operations of the grid, planning and exercising recovery operations, and continually expanding distributed power could significantly shorten the duration of any blackout and reduce economic and societal damage.

A SANS Institute report concluded that the effects of the attack on Ukraine's power grid were largely mitigated because grid operations there could be returned to manual control. Most experts believe that the current complexity of grid operations in the United States would make a switch to manual operations difficult; newer systems might not allow for the use of manual controls at all. Requiring the ability to shift to manual controls and exercising those controls on an annual basis might now be the most valuable step to take. Michael Assante, the former chief information security officer for NERC, argues that utilities should design their systems with backup tools that are either not connected to any information technology networks or are analog. For certain pieces of technology, it may make sense to replace software systems with hardware systems, hardwiring functions into circuit boards so that they cannot be modified remotely.

The next administrator of the Federal Emergency Management Agency (FEMA) could make response and recovery planning a priority. The all-hazards approach favored in emergency management may prove insufficient for a blackout of long duration covering large swaths of the nation. Beyond domestic emergency planning, exercising crisis response at a national level with government, allies, and private sector actors would be valuable. Doing so would identify the difficulties of operating without power systems and prompt the development of response options to prevent unneeded delay.

The continued expansion of distributed generation in the form of wind and solar installations could also significantly reduce the magnitude of an attack on the grid; however, most rooftop systems feed directly into the grid, and homes and businesses do not draw from their own systems. From a resiliency perspective, it might be worth incentivizing the purchase of systems that allow a direct draw and have on-site storage. Moving military installations in the continental United States off the grid so that they can supply their own power would eliminate one of the rationales for attacking the grid and limit the hindrance caused by such an attack on military operations.

Post-attack Measures

Following an attack, eliminating malware and regaining control of the power grid would likely be carried out by the owners and the operators of affected systems with support from private incident response teams. Specialized support from the Department of Homeland Security's Industrial Control System Computer Emergency Response Team (ICS-CERT) and the DOE national labs would also be provided.

The government's main role would be attributing the attack and responding to it. The FBI would take lead responsibility for investigating the attack domestically and for conducting computer forensics. The intelligence community would look at its existing intelligence collection for indications of what might have been missed and would begin targeted collection efforts to trace the attack. Within weeks, the U.S. government would have confidence in its attribution.

The White House would set the public posture for the response. Based on precedents from both cyber- and non-cyberattacks over multiple administrations, government agencies would likely advocate for a show of firm resolve but recommend avoiding a rush to judgment or an immediate counterattack. Agencies would present a range of options to respond. These options would include a show of military force, such as moving U.S. ships into disputed waters or staging exercises in contested regions; response in kind, through cyberspace; traditional military options; public and private diplomacy; use of economic sanctions targeting the state and the private entities or individuals involved; use of international law enforcement to arrest any parties involved; and targeting of known intelligence assets. The president should choose a strategy that combines these options in such a way as to deter the adversary from escalating further—the adversary should recognize that the consequences of continued escalation will be severe and choose to cease hostile activity, allowing a reset of the relationship.

RECOMMENDATIONS

The Donald J. Trump administration should focus its efforts on preventing an attack on the grid both through a deterrence policy and by strengthening security. The deterrence policy should articulate how the administration would view an attack on the power grid and should outline possible response options. As a starting point, the administration should be clear that an action against the grid would be treated as an armed attack and signal that a military response in or out of cyberspace would likely be required. The policy should also address how the administration would view the discovery that an adversary had taken initial steps toward a takedown of the grid, particularly the discovery that foreign actors had infiltrated utility networks. Together with continually demonstrating law enforcement and intelligence capabilities to attribute the sources of cyberattacks, a strong statement on deterrence could do more than anything else to prevent an attack on the grid. To ensure that the United States will be able to maintain military operations even in the face of a large blackout, the Trump administration should plan to end the reliance of military installations on the grid. Doing so would also reduce the likelihood of the grid becoming a military target.

To protect the grid from cyberattack, the Trump administration should initially focus on creating an information-sharing system that can bring together early signals that an attack against the grid is under way and share information that can be used to stop it. A stronger E-ISAC and a strong DOE counterpart to support it are necessary. The DOE should model its efforts on the Department of Defense's Cyber Crime Center, which provides intelligence feeds and forensic support to companies within the defense industrial base. The newly created Cyber Threat Intelligence Integration Center within the Office of the Director of National Intelligence should ensure that collection and analysis of threats to the grid are an intelligence priority and that intelligence on threats to the grid are downgraded and shared with targeted utilities.

In the event that an attack on the grid succeeds in causing blackout to some extent, the Trump administration should ensure that both the government and the industry are prepared to respond. FEMA should develop a response plan for a prolonged regional blackout that addresses the logistical difficulties of responding at scale in an environment degraded by the loss of power. NERC standards should require companies to maintain capabilities for manual operations. Those operations need to be exercised on a regional and coordinated basis.

Finally, the Trump administration should ensure that utilities can invest sufficiently in cybersecurity and do not need to make tradeoffs between traditional risk management activities and addressing national security threats. Increased funding could be achieved through a user fee similar to the universal service fee on phone lines, though a new tax on consumers may not be politically feasible. Alternatively, a tax deduction for utility spending on cybersecurity may be a less direct— but more politically palatable—way to increase funding. The Trump administration should also set security requirements for infrastructure investments made for the grid as part of its proposed stimulus package.

Collectively, these recommendations, if implemented, would greatly reduce the likelihood of an adversary deciding to conduct a cyberattack on the U.S. power grid while also improving the chances that the United States would manage any such attack without significant disruption of service.

AN ISRAELI STRIKE ON IRAN

Steven Simon

Successive Israeli governments have held that a nuclear weapons capability in the region, other than Israel's own, would pose an intolerable threat to Israel's survival as a state and society. Iran's nuclear program—widely regarded as an effort to obtain a nuclear weapon, or put Tehran "a turn of a screw" away from it—has triggered serious concern in Israel. Within the coming year, the Israeli government could decide, much as it did twenty-eight years ago with respect to Iraq and two years ago with respect to Syria, to attack Iran's nuclear installations in order to delay its acquisition of a weapons capability.

While U.S. officials—including the president—have declared a nuclear armed Iran to be "unacceptable," the administration has been clear in wanting to prevent such an outcome through peaceful diplomatic means. Without forswearing the eventual use of military force, senior U.S. officials have also indicated that a preventive strike on Iran by Israel would be "ill advised," "very destabilizing," and "likely very bad," and thus not in the U.S. interest. These concerns have evidently been transmitted privately to the Israeli government.

This contingency planning memo assesses the likelihood of an Israeli strike against Iran despite U.S. objections, the implications for the United States should it take place, the policy options available to reduce the chances of its occurrence, and the measures that could be taken to mitigate the potentially negative consequences.

This Contingency Planning Memorandum was originally published in November 2009. See Steven Simon, "An Israeli Strike on Iran," Council on Foreign Relations, November 2009, http://cfr.org/report/israeli-strike-iran.

THE CONTINGENCY

An Israeli attack would likely concentrate on three locations: Isfahan, where Iran produces uranium hexafluoride gas; Natanz, where the gas is enriched in approximately half of the eight thousand centrifuges located there; and Arak, where a heavy water research reactor, scheduled to come on line in 2012, would be ideal to produce weapons-grade plutonium. It is conceivable that Israel may attack other sites that it suspects to be part of a nuclear weapons program if targeting data were available, such as the recently disclosed Qom site, whose location is known, or centrifuge fabrication sites, the location(s) of which have not yet been identified. The latter would be compelling targets since their destruction would hobble Iran's ability to reconstitute its program. But attacks against the sites at Natanz, Isfahan, and Arak alone would likely stretch Israel's capabilities, and planners would probably be reluctant to enlarge the raid further.

Israel is capable of carrying out these attacks unilaterally. Its F-16 and F-15 aircraft, equipped with conformal fuel tanks and refueled with 707-based and KC-130 tankers toward the beginning and end of their flight profiles, have the range to reach the target set, deliver their payloads in the face of Iranian air defenses, and return to their bases. The munitions necessary to penetrate the targets are currently in Israel's inventory in sufficient numbers; they include Bomb Live Unit (BLU)-109 and BLU 113 bombs that carry two thousand and five thousand pounds, respectively, of high-energy explosives.

These GPS-guided weapons are extremely accurate and can be lofted from attacking aircraft fifteen kilometers from their target, thereby reducing the attackers' need to fly through air defenses. Israel also has a laser-guided version of these bombs that is more accurate than the GPS variant and could deploy a special-operations laser designation unit to illuminate aim points as it is reported to have done in the attack on the al-Kibar facility in Syria.

These munitions could be expected to damage the targets severely. Natanz is the only one of the three likely targets that is largely underground, sheltered by up to twenty-three meters of soil and concrete. BLU-type bombs, used in a "burrowing" mode, however, could penetrate deeply enough to fragment the inner surface of the ceiling structures above the highly fragile centrifuge arrays and even precipitate the collapse of the entire structure. Burrowing requires that attacking aircraft deliver their second and third bombs into the cavity created by the first. GPS-guided munitions are accurate enough to do this a little less than half of the time. The probability of successful burrowing increases with the number of shots. The use of three bombs per aim point would confer better than a 70 percent probability of success. (Laser-guided munitions are more capable of a successful burrow on the first try.) The uranium conversion facility in Isfahan and reactor at Arak are not buried and could be heavily damaged, or completely destroyed, relatively easily. This would be possible even if Iran managed to down a third of the Israeli strike package, a feat that would far exceed historical ratios of bomber losses by any country in any previous war.

These relatively upbeat ballistic assessments do not mean that the mission as a whole would be easy. On the contrary, a coordinated air attack would be complicated and highly risky. The three plausible routes to Iran involve overflight of third countries: the northern approach would likely follow the Syrian-Turkish border and risk violation of Turkey's airspace; the central flight path would cross Jordan and Iraq; a southern route would transit the lower end of Jordan, Saudi Arabia, and possibly Kuwait. All but two of these countries are to a greater or lesser degree hostile to Israel. The exceptions, Jordan and Turkey, would not wish their airspace to be used for an Israeli attack against Iran. Turkey recently canceled an annual trilateral exercise involving Israel, in part to signal its opposition to an Israeli strike. In any case, overflight would jeopardize Israeli diplomatic relations with both countries. With respect to Syria and Saudi Arabia, operational concerns would trump diplomatic ones. If either country detects Israeli aircraft and chooses to challenge the overflight using surface-to-air missiles or intercepting aircraft, Israel's intricate attack plan, which would have a razor-thin margin for error to begin with, could well be derailed.

Overflight of Iraq, whose airspace is under de facto U.S. control, would also be diplomatically awkward for Israel and would risk a deadly clash with American air defenses since the intruding aircraft would not have the appropriate Identification, Friend, or Foe (IFF) codes. Israel would have to carefully weigh the operational risk and most of all the cost of a strike to its most vital bilateral relationship, especially if President Barack Obama had explicitly asked Prime Minister Benjamin Netanyahu not to order an attack.

The sheer distances involved pose a challenge, as well. The targets lie at the outermost 1,750-kilometer range limits of Israeli tactical aircraft. Diplomatic and military factors would confine Israeli refueling operations to international airspace where tankers could orbit safely for long periods. These locations, while usable, are suboptimal. They would yield the attackers little leeway to loiter in their target areas, or engage in the fuel-intensive maneuvering typical of dogfights and evasion of surface-to-air missiles. The limited number of tankers would limit the number of sorties.

A final consideration for Israeli planners would be the effect of explosives on the nuclear materials stored at the uranium conversion facility at Isfahan and the enrichment facility at Natanz. Both facilities are likely to possess uranium hexafluoride and Natanz produces low enriched uranium. Though these materials are not radioactive and do not pose radiological risks, the release of uranium into the environment would almost certainly raise public health concerns due to heavy metal contamination.

This combination of diplomatic and operational complexities would clearly give Israeli leaders pause. To act, they would have to perceive a grave threat to the state of Israel and no reliable alternative to eliminating that threat.

ASSESSING THE LIKELIHOOD OF AN ISRAELI ATTACK

The likelihood of this contingency depends on Israeli assessments of U.S. and international resolve to block Iran's pursuit of a nuclear weapons capability; the state of the Iranian program; the amount of time a successful strike would buy to be worth the expected risks and costs, a point on which there is a spectrum of Israeli views, from six months to five years; whether Israel believes there is a clandestine Iranian program, which would lead some Israelis to conclude that an attack would not buy any time at all; and the effect of a strike on the U.S.-Israel relationship. Because none of these factors is constant, estimates about the likelihood of an Israeli strike within the coming year will vary. For example, Israel is probably somewhat less likely to attack now than it was before the Qom installation was disclosed, the P-3 took a firmer stance, and Russia appeared to concede that stronger sanctions had to be considered. If Iran were to agree to ship the bulk of its uranium to France and Russia for enrichment—a deal that has been agreed in working level negotiations but may never be consummated—Israel's incentive to accept the risks of an attack against Iran would probably diminish. Should diplomatic initiatives run aground, the likelihood of an Israeli attack could be expected to increase accordingly.

Probability assessments will vary based on other factors, as well. Iranian rhetoric that reinforces President Mahmoud Ahmadinejad's themes of Holocaust denial and the inevitable disappearance of Israel only strengthen the hand of attack proponents within Israel by justifying fears about Iran's intentions, while lowering diplomatic barriers to an attack. Certain factors that will not be publicly apparent could play a role, such as developments regarding Israel's overflight options that reduce the risks inherent in the mission; the availability to Israel of new, more accurate targeting intelligence, especially relating to single points of failure, or other potentially catastrophic vulnerabilities in Iran's installations; and technical advances, particularly in air defense suppression, that reduce the risks in attempting penetration.

It is clear, however, that Israel sees the stakes as very high. Netanyahu's UN General Assembly speech emphasized the existential nature of the threat that he and others in the current government believe Iran represents. His emphasis on the Holocaust as a defining feature of Jewish history and his self-conception as the one who bears the burden of preventing yet another such disaster suggest that U.S. calculations of risk and benefit that tilt toward Israeli restraint might prove to be mirror-imaging of a particularly deceptive sort. Given Iran's supportive relationship with certain terrorist groups in the region, Israel also cannot ignore the risk that a nuclear device might be transferred to them in the future. The longer-term impact of Iran acquiring nuclear weapons on triggering further proliferation in the Middle East, not least among states hostile to Israel, will also enter into their strategic calculus.

Israeli officials are aware that no conceivable Israeli strike could completely eliminate the nuclear threat posed by Iran and that an attack might only intensify longer-term risks as Iran reconstituted covertly, advancing an argument long made by counterterrorism officials that any effort to counter Iran's nuclear challenge is going to be like "mowing the lawn." Just as the grass will grow again, so will the nuclear program;

Israel will just have to mow again. And as Iran's reconstitution effort goes underground and its defenses are enhanced, Israel's intelligence and military capabilities will have to keep pace. They also argue, however, that the advantages of buying time should not be disregarded. Thus, the 1981 Osirak attack won two crucial decades during which Operation Desert Storm effectively disarmed Iraq and Operation Iraqi Freedom finally decapitated it. Neither tectonic event could have been predicted in 1981. (The counterargument is that the Osirak raid stimulated Iraq to switch to a highly enriched uranium [HEU] route and vastly increased the money and manpower devoted to the program. Whether or not the bombing set back Iraq's program, the point is that many Israelis believe that it did.) On this Israeli view, a strike might prove worthwhile in ways that neither Israel nor the United States can anticipate at this stage.

In assessing the likelihood of an attack, it is useful to look back on the origins of the Six Day War in 1967 and the raid on the Osirak reactor in Iraq. In each case, Israel attacked only after a long period of procrastination. In 1967, Washington's hands-off posture tipped the balance in the cabinet in favor of preemption. In the case of Osirak, the Carter and Reagan administrations' unwillingness or incapacity to intervene left Israel feeling cornered and compelled to act unilaterally. One lesson to be learned from this is that Israel is more likely to use force if it perceives Washington to be disengaged.

Finally, if the Russian analysis is correct—namely, that the sort of crippling sanctions that would help stave off an Israeli attack would also drive Iran out of the Nuclear Nonproliferation Treaty (NPT)—then the probability of an Israeli strike would be correspondingly higher, since Iranian withdrawal from the NPT would itself be a casus belli. Moreover, Iran's withdrawal would diminish the diplomatic opportunity cost of an attack.

WARNING INDICATORS

Surprise would be essential to the success of an attack and Israel's operational security would be correspondingly strong. Accordingly, tactical warning would be elusive. However, certain indicators have already surfaced; the appearance of others could indicate an Israeli intent to attack.

One indicator would be Israeli efforts to enhance the operational feasibility of the military option before a political decision to attack. Such actions would also serve the dual purpose of signaling Iran and others of Israel's resolve and capability with an eye to deterring further

Iranian movement toward a nuclear weapons capability. Recent developments in this category include the June 2008 long-range joint-air exercise—involving one hundred aircraft, long-range combat search and rescue helicopters, and refueling aircraft—which corresponded in scale and reach to an Israeli strike against Iran. The unprecedented June 2009 passage of an Israeli submarine through the Suez Canal, which showed that Israel had a maritime attack option in addition to air strikes, and that Jerusalem would have the support of at least one regional state, namely Egypt, represents another such signal. Similar indicators that might not be apparent outside of intergovernmental deliberations or the intelligence domain could include requests for targeting data and/or repositioning of strike aircraft within Israel once an attack path had been selected.

Other operational preparations could also portend Israeli action. These include bolstering homeland security, especially if it involves an emphasis on shelter locations, distribution of gas masks, or similar precautions against retaliatory attack. Tactical changes, including redeployment of ground forces to reinforce Israeli Northern Command and potentially enter Lebanon from a cold start, could also indicate a stronger likelihood of an Israeli attack.

Political developments inside Israel and Iran could also presage a decision to attack. For instance, broader public references to the Holocaust and warnings that time is running out would suggest an increasing probability of Israeli action. Netanyahu has sounded these themes regularly. If the political opposition echoed them, domestic political barriers to attack would have lowered.

Finally, delivery of advanced Russian S-300 surface to air missiles to Iran, which would multiply the risks of an air attack, might spur Israel to strike before the missiles were fielded.

POTENTIAL CONSEQUENCES FOR U.S. INTERESTS

Some observers would view an Israeli attack that significantly degraded Iran's nuclear weapons capability as beneficial to U.S. counterproliferation objectives and ultimately to U.S. national security. The United States has a clear interest in the integrity of the NPT regime and the compliance of member states with meaningful inspection arrangements. The use of force against Iran's nuclear program would, at a minimum, show that attempts to exploit the restraint of interested powers, manipulate the diplomatic process, game the NPT, and impede International Atomic Energy Agency (IAEA) access to nuclear-related facilities could carry serious penalties. Were Iran to acquire a nuclear weapons capability, the ability of the U.S. military forces to operate freely in the vicinity of Iran could, under some circumstances, be constrained. Looking into the future, a hostile Iran could also develop reliable long-range delivery systems for nuclear warheads that could strike American territory.

At the same time, an Israeli attack—even if operationally successful—would pose immediate risks to U.S. interests.

First, regardless of perceptions of U.S. complicity in the attack, the United States would probably become embroiled militarily in any Iranian retaliation against Israel or other countries in the region. Given uncertainties about the future of Iraq and a deepening commitment to Afghanistan, hostilities with Iran would stretch U.S. military capabilities at a particularly difficult time while potentially derailing domestic priorities.

Second, an Israeli strike would cause oil prices to spike and heighten concerns that energy supplies through the Persian Gulf may become disrupted. Should Iran attempt to block the Strait of Hormuz by mining, cruise missile strikes, or small boat attacks, these fears would become realized. According to the GAO, however, the loss of Iranian oil for eighteen months would increase prices by only $6 to $11/bbl, assuming that the International Energy Agency coordinated release of reserves. This said, at the onset of the crisis, prices might hit $200/bbl (up from the current level of around $77/bbl) for a short period but would likely quickly subside.

Third, since the United States would be viewed as having assisted Israel, U.S. efforts to foster better relations with the Muslim world would almost certainly suffer. The United States has an enduring strategic interest in fostering better relations with the Muslim world, which is distinct from the ruling elites on whom the United States depends for an array of regional objectives. In part, this interest derives from the need to lubricate cooperation between the United States and these governments by lowering some of the popular resentment of Washington that can hem in local leaders and impede their support for U.S. initiatives. A narrative less infused by anti-Americanism also facilitates counterterrorism goals and, from a longer-range perspective, hedges against regime change. The perceived involvement of the United States in an Israeli attack would undercut these interlocking interests, at least for a while.

Fourth, the United States has a strong interest in domestically generated regime change in Iran. Although some argue that the popular anger aroused in Iran by a strike would be turned against a discredited clerical regime that seemed to invite foreign attack after its bloody post-election repression of nonviolent opposition, it is more likely that Iranians of all stripes would rally around the flag. If so, the opposition Green movement would be undermined, while the ascendant hard-line clerics and Revolutionary Guard supporters would face fewer constraints in consolidating their hold on power.

Fifth, an Israeli attack might guarantee an overtly nuclear weapons capable Iran in the medium-term.

Sixth, although progress toward an Israeli-Palestinian final status accord remains elusive, an Israeli strike, especially one that overflew Jordan or Saudi Arabia, would delay fruitful renewed negotiation indefinitely. Both Washington and Jerusalem would be too preoccupied with managing the consequences of an attack, while regional capitals would deflect U.S. appeals to upgrade relations with Israel as an incentive to concessions. If Hamas or Hezbollah were to retaliate against Israel, either spontaneously or in response to Iranian pressure to act, any revival of the peace process would be further set back.

Finally, the United States has an abiding interest in the safety and security of Israel. Depending on the circumstances surrounding an Israeli attack, the political-military relationship between Jerusalem and Washington could fray, which could erode unity among Democrats and embolden Republicans, thereby complicating the administration's political situation, and weaken Israel's deterrent. Even if an Israeli move on Iran did not dislocate the bilateral relationship, it could instead produce diplomatic rifts between the United States and its European and regional allies, reminiscent of tensions over the Iraq war.

U.S. POLICY OPTIONS TO FORESTALL AN ISRAELI STRIKE

Assuming that the United States continues to assess an Israeli attack to be undesirable, options to forestall or hedge against a strike would have to be geared to negating factors that would lead Israel to assess that the benefits of an attack outweigh the costs. These factors include perceptions that the White House has given at least a yellow light to the strike; that the United States is disengaged either because it has run out of diplomatic options or because an agreement with Iran has met Washington's security objectives but left Israel exposed; and that the United States has not proffered to Israel convincing security guarantees against a nuclear-capable Iran. This list implies the importance of firm, direct communication of U.S. opposition to a strike from the White House to the Israeli prime minister; continued U.S. engagement that reflects an awareness of Israel's greater exposure to the Iranian threat relative to that of the United States; and a willingness to consider a palpable tightening of the U.S.-Israel strategic relationship that secures Israeli restraint and, conversely, warns of a rupture should Israel attack Iran despite the U.S. president's explicit opposition. If, over time, events develop in a way that, from a U.S. perspective, more fully warrants Israeli anxiety, the balance between warning and reassurance would of course shift, both privately and publicly.

To facilitate this new bilateral understanding, Washington could take any or all of the following preventive measures:

- Make progress toward a verifiable, highly transparent agreement with Iran that will make it very difficult to produce highly enriched uranium and/or weapons-grade plutonium, and secondarily to weaponize.

- Recreate the "Eagleburger Mission." In 1991, Deputy Secretary of State Lawrence Eagleburger led two small delegations to Israel when it was under Iraqi Scud attack. His objective was to urge Israeli restraint. The missions succeeded because the United States was firm in refusing Israeli access to Iraqi airspace, but worked with Israel on ways the United States could destroy the Scuds. The United States should establish a similar channel to Israel (if it has not been already) to gauge Israeli intentions and discuss steps to reduce the threat to Israel, while arguing that an Israeli military option would test the U.S.-Israel relationship without reducing the long-term Iranian threat. Other objectives would be to make clear that overflight of Iraq would not be permitted; share the U.S. assessment of the risks and potential costs of overflight of third countries; and explore Israeli expectations and response options about Iranian retaliation.

- Continue to declare the "unacceptable" nature of a nuclear Iran and that "all options remain on the table" to reassure Israel that the United States would not seek a diplomatic accommodation that compromised Israel's security.

- Send high-profile visitors to Israel on reassurance missions; a presidential visit to express solidarity with Israel and emphasize measures the United States is taking on the nuclear issue would be helpful.

- Extend to Israel the option of a defense treaty with the United States. Such a treaty would contain unambiguous security guarantees to Israel that it would be covered by the U.S. "nuclear umbrella" so as to deter Iran. Although it is unclear whether Israel would welcome such a treaty, other states that felt threatened by Iran's acquisition of nuclear weapons, notably Egypt and Saudi Arabia, would likely demand similar coverage if it were extended to Israel.

Finally, the United States could also consider the option advocated by former national security adviser Zbigniew Brzezinski, that of the United States actively impeding an Israeli attack once it is under way. It is hard to imagine, however, that the United States would risk the severe—even permanent—damage such action would incur on its long-standing strategic relationship with Israel.

U.S. POLICY OPTIONS TO MITIGATE/MANAGE A CRISIS

While doing all it can to forestall an Israeli attack, the United States must also plan for managing and minimizing the crisis that would ensue if the primary policy fails and Israel does in fact attack Iran. Such planning should include the following steps:

- work with basing countries—especially Bahrain, Qatar, and the United Arab Emirates (UAE)—on first response, consequence management capacities, and intelligence exchanges;

- ramp up air defenses and force protection in the Gulf and Iraq;

- discuss the possibility of Iranian retaliation and responses with Iraqi president Nuri al-Maliki and senior Iraqi security officials;

- approach Saudi Arabia, the UAE, and Kuwait with requests to increase oil production should Iran attempt to block the Strait of Hormuz, attack shipping, or damage transloading facilities or offshore installations;

- ensure the U.S. Strategic Petroleum Reserve is sufficient to offset shortages if necessary;

- use diplomatic and intelligence channels to urge increased readiness levels in friendly countries where there is an Iranian Revolutionary Guard or a Hezbollah presence; and

- provide additional ballistic missile defense capabilities to Israel to defend against potential Iranian retaliation.

RECOMMENDATIONS

Israeli leaders have stated repeatedly that the problem posed by Iran's pursuit of mastery over the nuclear fuel cycle was the responsibility of the international community. For straightforward diplomatic reasons, Israel has not wanted the problem to be seen as Israel's alone. Such a perception would essentially permit important players to abandon the field, leaving Israel to cope with a threat that many believe to be existential. While the historical record shows Israel will act in the face of such a threat, there is a keen awareness among Israelis that the use of force would carry profound risks and, potentially, be open-ended. Room exists, therefore, for the United States to persuade Israel to exercise restraint. This goal will require a delicate balance of caution and reassurance.

As a first step, the United States and Israel should establish a high-level back channel to explore the issues raised by Iran's behavior and share views about managing them. Diplomacy, even secret diplomacy, does not necessarily entail total self-disclosure. But the situation demands frank discussion. As close allies exposed unequally to a consequential threat, conducting it will not be easy. There will be contentious issues, including definition of red lines and the comprehensiveness of U.S. assurances necessary to win the cooperation of a close ally boxed in by an indispensable patron and an implacable enemy. Above all, Israel must not be left to feel alone. Accordingly, the second step will be to maintain the cohesion of the five permanent members of the UN Security Council, plus Germany (the 5 + 1) that have taken the lead in diplomatic efforts, and to keep up the pressure on Iran. Simultaneously, the United States must hedge against the failure of a war-avoidance policy, and begin preparing for an Israeli attack on Iran and Iranian retaliation. This will be a thorny process insofar as defensive measures the United States takes in the region, or urges its allies to take, could be read in Tehran as preparation for an attack and thus cast as justification for further destabilizing Iranian action.

Israel is not eager for war with Iran, or to disrupt its special relationship with the United States. But the fact remains that it considers the Iranian threat an existential one and its bilateral relationship with the United States a durable one, and will act if it perceives momentous jeopardy to the Israeli people or state. Thus, while Israel may be amenable to American arguments for restraint, those arguments must be backed predominantly by concrete measures to contain the threat and reaffirmations of the special relationship, and only secondarily by warnings of the deterioration of the relationship, to be persuasive.

AVERTING A CROSS-STRAIT CRISIS

Michael S. Chase

The risk of a serious crisis between China and Taiwan is growing. Cross-strait relations have chilled in recent years as a result of the unwillingness of Taiwan's President Tsai Ing-wen to embrace the so-called 1992 Consensus—an understanding that was the basis for a warmer relationship between Beijing and Taipei under Tsai's predecessor, Ma Ying-jeou of the Kuomintang (KMT). According to the KMT, the 1992 Consensus holds that both mainland China and Taiwan belong to "one China" but with distinct interpretations. Beijing's stance, however, is that the 1992 Consensus means there is "one China," which is the People's Republic of China (PRC), and that Taiwan is part of the PRC. China responded to Tsai's refusal to endorse its approach to the 1992 Consensus by implementing a multifaceted pressure campaign to punish and coerce Taiwan into being more compliant. Beijing's tactics have included suspending official and semiofficial mechanisms for cross-strait communications, reducing the number of mainland tourists allowed to visit Taiwan, pressuring countries that recognize Taiwan to sever diplomatic relations with the island, and conducting military exercises and information operations designed to intimidate Taiwan.

This pressure campaign could intensify in the next twelve to eighteen months—particularly in the lead-up to and immediately following Taiwan's 2020 presidential election—to the extent that it triggers a new cross-strait crisis. Although the United States maintains a "one China"

This Contingency Planning Memorandum was originally published in February 2019. See Michael S. Chase, "Averting a Cross-Strait Crisis," Council on Foreign Relations, February 2019, http://cfr.org/report/averting-cross-strait-crisis.

policy in accordance with the three U.S.-China joint communiques and withdrew from its 1954 defense treaty with Taiwan after establishing diplomatic relations with the PRC in 1979, such a crisis would clearly affect U.S. national security interests.

Taiwan and the United States maintain an unofficial relationship, but the island is an important U.S. economic and security partner that shares democratic values. The 1979 Taiwan Relations Act holds that U.S. policy is "to consider any effort to determine the future of Taiwan by other than peaceful means, including by boycotts or embargoes, a threat to the peace and security of the Western Pacific area and of grave concern to the United States." Given its long-standing commitments to the security of Taiwan and its broader economic, diplomatic, and security interests in the Indo-Pacific, the United States would almost certainly become embroiled in a new cross-strait crisis. The United States should be attentive, therefore, to the potential direction of events and take steps to help avert and, if necessary, mitigate a new cross-strait confrontation.

THE CONTINGENCY

Three broad developments are increasing the risk of a cross-strait crisis in the coming months. The first relates to the important role domestic politics play in China and the potential calculations of the leadership. During a January 2019 speech marking the fortieth anniversary of the mainland's 1979 "Message to Compatriots in Taiwan," President Xi Jinping stated that unification with Taiwan is "a must for the great rejuvenation of the Chinese nation in the new era." President Xi has staked his political fortunes and personal legacy on realizing the "Chinese dream" of "national rejuvenation," especially in the context of the approaching centenaries of the Chinese Communist Party in 2021 and of the People's Republic in 2049. Xi has not set a deadline for China's unification with Taiwan, but it is an important part of this policy agenda and it is clearly linked to the realization of these broader strategic goals. This approach could result in a China that is more assertive and willing to tolerate more risks in cross-strait relations. A slowing economy might also tempt Xi to try to resolve the Taiwan question to bolster his legitimacy at home. Additionally, changing perceptions within China of the regional military dynamics and growing confidence in the capabilities of the People's Liberation Army (PLA), or doubts about U.S. willingness and ability to intervene on behalf of Taiwan, could embolden China to exercise its leverage over Taiwan more aggressively,

potentially leading to the most serious crisis in the cross-strait relationship in more than two decades.

The second development is that political trends in Taiwan are
moving in a direction unfavorable to China's point of view. People
in Taiwan increasingly see themselves as Taiwanese rather than Chinese, according to recent polling data. In June 2018, the Election Study
Center at National Chengchi University in Taipei found that 55.8 percent of people in Taiwan view themselves as Taiwanese, up from 17.6
percent in 1992, while the number of people identifying as Chinese
has declined to 3.5 percent (37.2 percent identify as both Taiwanese
and Chinese). There is little support in Taiwan for China's "one country, two systems" approach, and the heavy-handed implementation
of such a system in Hong Kong is making it even more unattractive to
people in Taiwan. While the opposition KMT outperformed the ruling
Democratic Progressive Party (DPP) in Taiwan's November 2018
local elections, most observers of the elections attribute this result to
the economy and other domestic factors rather than Tsai's cross-strait
policies. In November 2018, following the DPP's defeat in the local
elections, Tsai resigned as chair of the party and was replaced in January 2019 by Cho Jung-tai. Critics have called for a different candidate
to serve as the DPP's standard-bearer for the presidential election in
2020, opening up the possibility for a more pro-independence candidate to run, but Cho is a moderate ally of Tsai, making it less likely that
she will face a serious internal challenge. Although Tsai has pursued a
relatively cautious course toward the mainland—certainly in contrast
to the 2000–2008 policies of Taiwan's first DPP president, Chen Shui-
bian—after Xi's January 2019 speech, she has publicly used tougher
language, which appears to have helped strengthen her political position. She could employ more assertive rhetoric during the 2020 presidential election in response to growing pressure from China.

The third development is that U.S. policy toward Taiwan is changing
in a way that China perceives as more antagonistic, especially against the
backdrop of deteriorating U.S.-China relations. Beijing was alarmed by
then President-Elect Donald J. Trump's phone call with President Tsai.
Since then, the U.S. Congress has passed the 2018 Taiwan Travel Act,
which encourages high-level U.S. officials to visit Taiwan, much to China's displeasure. The Trump administration has also openly declared
China to be a geopolitical rival and a revisionist power, and has imposed
trade tariffs against many Chinese products and sanctions against the
Equipment Development Department of China's Central Military

Commission. The U.S. Navy, moreover, has increased the number of freedom of navigation operations in the South China Sea to challenge China's maritime claims. In addition, the U.S. Navy conducted three Taiwan Strait transits in 2018.

Specific events related to one or more of those developments could prompt China to intensify its pressure campaign against Taiwan. This could include, for example, a decision by Xi to press for cross-strait negotiations on an accelerated timetable, Tsai's replacement ahead of Taiwan's 2020 election by a candidate more interested in independence, or an attempt by the United States to demonstrate its support for Taiwan that inadvertently prompts Chinese escalation.

Whatever the triggering event or sequence of events, China could choose a variety of responses, either separately or in combination.

- *Diplomatic isolation.* China could try to further decrease Taiwan's diplomatic space by targeting several of Taiwan's seventeen remaining diplomatic allies simultaneously. For example, China could try to further decrease Taiwan's diplomatic space by pressuring those countries that still officially recognize Taipei to switch their ties to Beijing. This includes the Vatican and Eswatini, Taiwan's only remaining diplomatic partners in Europe and Africa respectively, as well as nine states in Latin America and the Caribbean and six in the Pacific. Beijing could also try strong-arming some of Taipei's unofficial partners into curtailing their level of interaction with Taiwan.

- *Economic coercion.* China could sharply increase economic pressure on Taiwan. For instance, Beijing could stop most or all mainland tourists from visiting the island, reduce the number of mainland students in Taiwan, or harass Taiwanese businesses in China as it did South Korean businesses over the deployment of the Terminal High Altitude Area Defense (THAAD) missile system in 2017.

- *Military intimidation.* China has numerous options to display military power in an attempt to intimidate Taiwan. The PLA could hold major military exercises opposite Taiwan. Such exercises could include a demonstration of amphibious landing capabilities. China could also dramatically increase the level of air force and naval activity around Taiwan, for instance by dispatching its aircraft carrier and conducting flight operations close to Taiwan. China could send fighter aircraft or reconnaissance aircraft across the Taiwan Strait centerline to send a message to Taiwan. In addition, China could increase the number of

H-6K bomber flights around Taiwan, which the former sometimes refers to as "encirclement patrols." At a higher level of intensity, China could conduct missile flight tests close to Taiwan as it did in the 1995–96 crisis, or even launch a missile over the island.

- *Influence operations.* China could increase its use of official media channels or social media platforms to amplify the message sent by other types of coercive activity. Additionally, China could launch a major information operations campaign against Taiwan, one that could exceed the scale and scope of what it has done in recent years. A stepped-up campaign could include activities such as funding or providing other forms of clandestine support to actors that back Beijing's agenda, hacking and releasing emails of political actors, and increasing social media manipulation to undermine confidence in the integrity of elections or sow division in Taiwan more generally.

Such tactics would conceivably set in motion a series of cross-strait interactions that could escalate tensions to dangerous levels. Much will hinge on how policymakers in the United States, China, and Taiwan perceive and understand one another's motivations, something that could prove difficult. For instance, it might be hard for Washington and Taipei to tell whether Beijing's aims are relatively limited (i.e., to coerce Taiwan into again accepting the 1992 Consensus) or if China aims to fundamentally change the cross-strait relationship and push Taiwan in a direction more conducive to realizing Xi's long-term "national rejuvenation" goals.

Compounding this problem, decision-makers may be unable to correctly interpret the strategic signals sent by the other parties in a growing test of wills. For example, it could be difficult for the United States to ascertain whether a particular movement of military forces by China is intended as a deterrence message or is indicative of an impending escalation of the crisis. China might have similar difficulties interpreting signals sent by the United States. Potentially complicating the situation, the departure of U.S. troops from Syria and possibly from Afghanistan—coupled with the United States' perceived failure to honor other commitments—could tempt China to increase the pressure on Taiwan, as party leaders may interpret such developments as an indication that the Trump administration would be reluctant to respond as forcefully as his predecessors would have been. As a result, once tensions rise, the relevant parties may be unable to calibrate their responses in ways that would advance their interests while limiting the risk of inadvertent escalation.

Various warning indicators are associated with each of the three con-tributing developments to a cross-strait crisis discussed above. For domestic developments in Taiwan, the most obvious relate to Tsai's statements, the approval ratings of the DPP ahead of the next elections, changing public opinion (particularly in relation to China), and the emergence of a more pro-independence DPP candidate or a surprise third-party candidate ahead of the 2020 election. The possibility of a DPP candidate Beijing distrusts even more than Tsai, or of a three-way race for the presidency in 2020, could create unpredictable dynamics.

The warning indicator associated with Beijing's desire to ramp up the pressure campaign against Taipei would be sharper rhetoric from Xi, which could indicate impatience with Taiwan or serve as a warning that there could be consequences if Beijing perceives Taipei as politically moving further away from the mainland. Xi could signal an impending increase in pressure by using new language suggesting urgency about Taiwan, such as setting an explicit timetable for unifica-tion. Alternatively, he could repeat his previous statement suggesting that the issue of Taiwan should not be passed down from "generation to generation," or his earlier warning that if the foundation of the cross-strait relationship erodes "the earth will move, and the moun-tains will shake." Although a surprise attack by China is extremely unlikely, Xi could also attempt to send a message to Taiwan and the United States by highlighting the PLA's preparedness for conflict across the Taiwan Strait. For example, Xi could declare the ongoing PLA reforms and reorganization a success. China is undoubtedly aware that some observers suspect the PLA would not be ready for a major conflict in the short term because of the ongoing restructuring, so signaling that the PLA is ready (or that it would be by 2020) could be a seen as a warning.

Changes in U.S. policy or a further deterioration of the U.S.-China relationship could also provide warning indicators. If the United States were to take action that suggests it could fundamentally redefine its policy toward Taiwan or abandon its long-standing "one China" policy, China would likely respond strongly. Short of such a dramatic alteration to U.S. policy, if Washington proceeds with actions that Beijing sees as emboldening leaders in Taipei to reject the mainland's demands or to move further in a direction that China views as anti-thetical to its interests, the risk of a cross-strait crisis could increase.

For example, China strongly objected to the 2018 Taiwan Travel Act, which states that Congress believes it should be U.S. policy to allow U.S. officials at all levels to visit Taiwan. Chinese commentators have also expressed concern about calls for Taiwan to be invited to participate in the Rim of the Pacific (RIMPAC) military exercise and for U.S. Navy vessels to make port calls in Taiwan. A high-profile arms sale to Taiwan that included cutting-edge hardware such as F-35 fighters or submarines could also raise tensions with China. Additionally, a sharp downturn in the U.S.-China relationship over other issues, such as trade or the South China Sea, could make a cross-strait crisis more likely by hardening Chinese perceptions that the United States is intent on containing China and wishes to play the Taiwan card to check China's rise more broadly.

If China decides, for whatever reason, to ramp up pressure on Taiwan, there would likely be additional signals including leadership statements that criticize specific actions by Taiwan or the United States, harsh condemnations of pro-independence politicians in Taiwan in various media outlets, and other moves to prepare the public for a confrontation. In addition, some tactical indicators might be observable shortly before China increases the pressure on Taiwan. These signs could include unusual activity by Chinese military units, intensified intelligence operations against Taiwan, or heightened levels of Chinese computer espionage against political parties or election-related targets in Taiwan.

IMPLICATIONS FOR U.S. INTERESTS

A cross-strait crisis in the run-up to Taiwan's 2020 elections or shortly after would present serious risks to U.S. interests.

At a minimum, a cross-strait crisis could result in a broader freeze in U.S.-China relations, which could complicate other important issues—regionally and globally—in the relationship. For example, it could exacerbate tensions in other areas where there is already considerable friction (e.g., maritime disputes in the South China Sea) or imperil cooperation on other issues of concern (e.g., North Korean denuclearization), at least temporarily. A successful pressure campaign could embolden China to apply similar tactics elsewhere. For example, if the Chinese government successfully intensified its interference in Taiwan's elections (e.g., social media manipulation, covert financing of preferred candidates, or hacking and releasing emails or other data), it could try to apply the same or similar tactics elsewhere.

A crisis could also fundamentally damage U.S.-China relations and the overall U.S. posture in the Indo-Pacific. This scenario could play out differently depending on how the United States reacts and how its reaction is perceived by other actors in the region. Particularly if the U.S.-China relationship continues to be characterized by friction over trade and security issues, a concerted U.S. effort to push back on Chinese pressure could convince Beijing that Washington views Taipei as a useful part of a containment strategy. On the one hand, the consequences for U.S.-China relations could be severe, potentially solidifying a more adversarial relationship overall, but U.S. allies and partners might be reassured by a demonstration of Washington's willingness and ability to stand up to Beijing. On the other hand, if the United States fails to help Taiwan respond to escalating Chinese pressure tactics or if the United States responds but is unable to stop China, other U.S. allies and partners in the Indo-Pacific—in particular Japan and South Korea—might see the United States as lacking in resolve or in capability. This scenario could increase their concerns about Washington's reliability and predictability, and cast doubt on the credibility of U.S. commitments in the region and beyond—all of which would undermine Washington's ability to implement national security and national defense strategies that rely on cooperation with allies and partners.

Finally, although the risk of a crisis escalating to war is low—as that outcome is presumed not to be in any actor's interest—it exists. Misunderstandings and miscalculation could still propel the parties to outright conflict.

PREVENTIVE OPTIONS

The United States has several preventive options to try to avoid another cross-strait crisis. These options include the following:

- *Encourage Beijing and Taipei to avoid a breakdown in cross-strait relations.* Washington could encourage Beijing and Taipei to improve their channels of communication in hopes of avoiding a breakdown in cross-strait ties. The United States could also caution both sides to avoid unilateral actions that could further deteriorate the situation, as President George W. Bush did in 2003 over concerns about then President Chen's referendum plans. The situation has since changed, and the current threat to stability comes primarily from the mainland. Tsai has been largely pragmatic since assuming office, but Beijing appears to distrust her and has increased the pressure on Taipei because it is unwilling to accept an outcome short of an endorsement of the 1992 Consensus and its core connotation of "one China." A more ambitious version of such an approach could also include encouraging the mainland and Taiwan to search for creative ways to break the current impasse, such as finding an alternative to the 1992 Consensus that is acceptable to leaders on both sides. However, the chances of success are slim. Moreover, given the recent deterioration in the U.S.-China relationship, Beijing would likely reject any such U.S. involvement as interference aimed at undermining China's interests. In addition, many people in Taiwan might object to such a U.S. initiative, seeing it as pressure to accommodate China and thus a potential violation of long-standing U.S. assurances.

- *Strengthen the U.S.-Taiwan relationship and enhance Taiwan's resilience.* The United States could enhance its support for Taiwan within the framework of its long-standing policy approach, helping improve Taiwan's resilience and strengthen its deterrence posture vis-à-vis China. This support could include new arms sales, and perhaps further normalization of the arms sales process, but it need not be limited to military hardware. It could also include increasing assistance in other areas, such as strengthening Taiwan's reserve forces and helping Taiwan develop a more innovative defense strategy. Washington might also consider being more transparent about some aspects of U.S.-Taiwan security cooperation in order to more clearly signal its support for Taipei. Furthermore, while some may consider it hypocritical, Washington could also encourage Taipei's remaining diplomatic partners to resist pressure from the mainland to switch recognition to Beijing and step up its efforts to help Taiwan expand its international participation more generally. The United States could also facilitate Taiwan's efforts to diversify its economic relationships, such as by moving ahead with a U.S.-Taiwan trade agreement or by helping Taiwan join the Comprehensive and Progressive Agreement for Trans-Pacific Partnership (CPTPP). Additionally, the United States could help Taiwan improve its capacity to uncover and respond to China's cyber intrusions and political influence operations.

- *Strengthen U.S. capabilities for deterrence and the defense of Taiwan.* The United States could continue to develop advanced military capabilities and new operational concepts intended to prevent China from using force to compel unification. In addition, the United States could strengthen its deterrence of China by revealing enough about the development of these capabilities and concepts to demonstrate that it can respond effectively to any Chinese attempt to achieve unification by force. China's growing power means the United States will be unable to dominate China militarily, but it can still improve its ability to deter Chinese use of force and to defend Taiwan if deterrence fails.

MITIGATING OPTIONS

If China intensifies pressure on Taiwan ahead of the island's 2020 elections, a number of mitigating options would be available to U.S. policymakers to help avert and deescalate a crisis. These options include the following:

- *Seek to defuse the crisis diplomatically.* Washington could attempt to facilitate communication between Beijing and Taipei and encourage leaders on both sides of the Taiwan Strait to deescalate the situation and seek a cooperative, mutually acceptable way to end the crisis. Such an approach has several downsides. China might misread U.S. attempts to facilitate a cooperative resolution as reflecting weakness, particularly if they are not accompanied by signals of U.S. support for Taiwan and appropriate deterrence messages. In addition, the United States would need to be careful to avoid creating the perception that it is willing to ignore the wishes of the people of Taiwan, pressure Taiwan to accede to Chinese demands, or use Taiwan as a bargaining chip. Rather than pursue any breakthroughs, the United States could simply try to avoid any major breakdowns. To this end, the United States could signal its opposition to unilateral statements or actions by either China or Taiwan that would threaten further escalation of the situation, while avoiding any such statements or actions itself.

- *Demonstrate U.S. economic, military, and political support for Taiwan.* The United States could make clear that it supports Taiwan and intends to help the island withstand Chinese pressure. This option would need to be tailored to respond to China's approach. For example, if Chinese pressure against Taiwan involves information warfare or influence operations, the United States could provide technical expertise or other forms of assistance to help Taiwan assess and counter China's activities. Washington could also consider enlisting the assistance of other allies to show their support for Taipei. Even as it seeks to demonstrate its support for Taiwan, the United States would need to carefully avoid taking actions that might inadvertently escalate the crisis, such as deploying U.S. forces to Taiwan.

- *Take steps to persuade China to back down.* The United States could pressure China to back down or at least attempt to deter China from further escalating the crisis. This could include deploying additional military forces to the Indo-Pacific region to deter China. Washington could encourage some of its allies and partners to participate in these deterrence operations. The United States could also focus on influencing China's decision-making calculus by highlighting the risk that Beijing would be unable to control the pace of escalation or ensure a quick resolution of any conflict on acceptable terms, both through private channels and in public statements. At the same time, however, successfully persuading China to back down would almost certainly require some corresponding assurances that exercising restraint would not leave it in an unacceptable position. This option could be a challenge, however, as Beijing might not find the assurances credible, or Taipei might view them as potentially undermining its interests.

RECOMMENDATIONS

The situation across the Taiwan Strait is changing for several reasons, and the danger of a crisis appears to be growing as Taiwan's 2020 elections approach. Washington should aim to strengthen deterrence while working within the context of a long-standing policy that helps maintain stability and affords considerable flexibility.

Within this context, the United States is unlikely to facilitate a major breakthrough in cross-strait relations, though it should do what it can to prevent them from worsening. Because this is a sensitive time in cross-strait relations, careful diplomacy and stewardship are required to reduce the risk of crisis. In particular, the United States should encourage China and Taiwan to maintain a stable and constructive cross-strait relationship on terms consistent with the interests and aspirations of the people of Taiwan, primarily by reiterating clearly and publicly its opposition to unilateral actions altering the status quo. Unlike a decade ago, however, the U.S. response will need to take into account that unilateral action by the mainland appears to be a much greater threat than Taiwan's crossing a line that triggers a Chinese response.

The United States should also develop a multidimensional approach to enhancing its relationship with Taiwan and strengthening Taiwan's resilience and ability to deter Chinese coercion, as detailed below. Because escalating Chinese pressure presents a multifaceted threat to Taiwan, the United States should think more broadly about how to help

Taiwan strengthen deterrence and increase its resilience. Since Beijing would likely rely on a strategy that incorporates a variety of diplomatic, economic, military, and informational instruments of power, Washington should develop an approach that accounts for the challenges presented by all of the different elements of a Chinese coercion campaign against Taiwan. The overall goals should be to help Taiwan mitigate its vulnerabilities and to convince China that it would be unable to use its leverage against Taiwan in any of these areas without taking large risks.

To counter Chinese diplomatic isolation, the United States should continue to support Taiwan's participation in international organizations such as the International Civil Aviation Organization, Interpol, and the World Health Organization, and expand successful initiatives such as the Global Cooperation and Training Framework. The United States should also do more to facilitate Taiwan's efforts to deepen strategic dialogues and exchanges with other democracies, including Australia and Japan.

To bolster Taiwan's deterrence posture, the United States should continue arms sales to Taiwan and assist Taiwan in its attempts to strengthen its domestic defense industry. The United States should also enhance support for Taiwan's efforts to develop and implement a new defense strategy, strengthen its reserve forces, and reform its military service system. In return, the United States should expect Taiwan to increase its defense spending and focus on implementation of its new Overall Defense Concept, which emphasizes asymmetric responses to China's growing military power, including more mobile and survivable systems.

The United States should also aid Taiwan's efforts to diversify its economic relationships and reduce its economic dependence on China. This effort could include supporting President Tsai's New Southbound Policy, which is intended to enhance Taiwan's economic ties with the Association of Southeast Asian Nations (ASEAN), Australia, New Zealand, and South Asian states. In addition, it could include pursuing a U.S.-Taiwan trade agreement or supporting Taiwan's desire to participate in CPTPP.

The United States should explore additional ways to help Taiwan increase its ability to uncover and counter Chinese information warfare and political influence operations. Some of this help might need to be provided behind the scenes for it to be effective, but when possible the United States should consider publicizing what it knows about Chinese operations and publicly highlighting its willingness and ability to work with Taiwan to diminish their damage. The United States should also encourage other countries that have experience in countering Chinese or Russian influence operations, such as Australia and France, to coordinate and work with Taiwan to help build its capacity to respond to such activities.

The United States should further strengthen its own deterrence and defense capabilities and emphasize a deterrence-by-denial approach against China. This approach would likely be more credible than a deterrence approach that is premised on the threat of punishment and would also ensure that the United States is prepared to defend Taiwan if deterrence fails. Moreover, Washington should clearly communicate to Beijing that it is updating its own operational concepts and military capabilities in response to improvements in Chinese military power. Specifically, the United States should display new capabilities and conduct exercises in ways that are designed to show China that the United States will be able to counter Chinese use of force against Taiwan, if necessary. In addition, Washington should try to induce caution on Beijing's part by signaling that China would be unable to ensure a fast and decisive resolution on its terms, or to control escalation with the level of confidence some Chinese strategists have suggested would be the case in the event of a regional conflict.

The danger of a new cross-strait crisis is increasing as a result of developments in the United States, China, and Taiwan. A Taiwan Strait crisis could begin in several ways, and any such crisis would present serious challenges to U.S. interests. The risks would be heightened by the fact that Beijing has a wider and more powerful variety of options to coerce Taipei than it did during the last major showdown in 1995–96. Rather than waiting for the situation to deteriorate before taking action, U.S. policymakers should consider and prepare to implement options to avert a cross-strait crisis, as well as to be better positioned to deal with one effectively if it cannot be avoided.

POLITICAL INSTABILITY IN ZIMBABWE

George F. Ward

Political instability and potential violence could threaten Zimbabwe in the coming twelve to eighteen months. Zimbabwe's ninety-one-year-old president, Robert Mugabe, has no clear succession plan, and considerable uncertainty exists about whether a stable succession will take place. Zimbabwe's economy remains weak and vulnerable to potential shocks that might precipitate political instability as well. At the same time, government suppression of fundamental freedoms continues. Past crises have produced waves of refugees that have burdened Zimbabwe's neighbors. Renewed instability in Zimbabwe would be a special challenge for South Africa, which is attempting to deal with its own pressing economic and social needs. It would also set back U.S. interests in southern Africa, which are focused on support of good governance, trade, and investment. Alongside these risks, a post-Mugabe transition could present opportunities to begin to reverse the effects of decades of misrule in Zimbabwe. The United States should position itself to take advantage of these opportunities by working with others, notably South Africa and the other countries of the southern African region, to limit the risk of civil violence in Zimbabwe and to lay the groundwork for a better future.

THE CONTINGENCY

The risk factors associated with political instability in Zimbabwe are growing. Although President Mugabe has moved to strengthen his

---

This Contingency Planning Memorandum was originally published in March 2015. See George F. Ward, "Political Instability in Zimbabwe," Council on Foreign Relations, March 2015, http://cfr.org/report/political-instability-zimbabwe.

already tight grip on the levers of power within both the government and the ruling Zimbabwe African National Union-Patriotic Front (ZANU-PF), doubts remain as to how long tight discipline will last. Following the ZANU-PF party congress held December 2–7, 2014, Mugabe ousted Joice Mujuru from the vice presidency of both the party and the government, installing former Justice Minister Emmerson Mnangagwa in her place. Although Mnangagwa is widely seen as having gained an important advantage, the identity of Mugabe's successor remains an open question. Mugabe may serve out his term and successfully hand off power to an anointed successor, but events may unfold in a less orderly fashion. Acute instability in Zimbabwe could emerge at any time and play out along one or more of the three following lines:

Mugabe Dies or Becomes Incapacitated Before Installing a Chosen Successor

Mugabe's most imminent challenges are his advanced age and poor health. He has traveled abroad repeatedly for medical treatment of an undisclosed ailment. Despite this, Mugabe appears vigorous, maintains an active domestic and international schedule, and insists that he will run again for president in 2018. He was also elected in August 2014 to chair of the Southern African Development Community (SADC)—an intergovernmental organization that promotes economic, political, and security cooperation—and assumed the leadership of the African Union in January 2015.

In the past, Mugabe has treated his vice president as a figurehead rather than as a successor, and he seems to be continuing that practice even since the party congress. Mnangagwa has taken care of routine state functions during Mugabe's absences, but not the more important ZANU-PF party responsibilities. If this pattern continues, Mnangagwa will have limited opportunity to cement the loyalties he would need to rely on to succeed to the presidency. That failure could portend serious instability should Mugabe die or become incapacitated.

Mugabe's Control Is Challenged and Undermined by Growing Factionalism

The ZANU-PF won a resounding victory in the July 2013 national elections, and the opposition Movement for Democratic Change (MDC) is demoralized and somewhat discredited. Nevertheless, the run-up to the party congress demonstrated that factionalism is far from dead within the ruling party. The potential for intraparty strife may have increased as the result of the purge of former Vice President Mujuru, several of her loyal cabinet ministers, and large numbers of party and government officials at the regional and local levels. In dismissing Mujuru and her supporters—who at one point enjoyed majority support at the local level—Mugabe ran roughshod over electoral rules, made all significant decisions on his own, and dispensed with the facade of democratic procedures.

Mugabe will use his security apparatus to control the resentments and grievances of those who lost their offices and to provide the accompanying material benefits, but that dissent could boil over. Mujuru's allies have already filed a legal challenge to Mugabe's recent actions. Even in the likely event that the challenge goes nowhere in the courts, it symbolizes the open wound that exists in the ZANU-PF.

As the drama within the ZANU-PF plays out, President Mugabe will continue to play the dominant role, but the parts played by the current and former vice presidents, Mnangagwa and Mujuru, and by the first lady, Grace Mugabe, will bear close watching. Vice President Mnangagwa takes every opportunity to display his loyalty to Mugabe, sometimes even kneeling before him, but he has fallen into disfavor with Mugabe in the past. Historically, Mugabe's deputies have not fared well. Former Vice President Mujuru, the apparent major loser in the party congress and its aftermath, should not be counted out. She has strong support at the local and regional levels within the party, and she has significant ties to the security establishment on the basis both of her own record in the liberation conflict and that of her late husband, former army chief of staff Solomon Mujuru. Grace Mugabe is a wild card. Until the fall of 2014, she had occupied herself principally with tending the family's business interests. During the run-up to the party congress, she became hyperactive, waging a campaign against Mujuru, but also promoting her own role. Most observers believe that Grace Mugabe sees Mnangagwa as her future patron and protector, but others believe Mrs. Mugabe has ambitions to succeed her husband.

An Economic Crisis Triggers Demands for Political Change

Zimbabwe may be increasingly isolated from the West, but it is not insulated from the world economy. Bad economic news seems baked into Zimbabwe's future. Commodity prices have declined and a turnaround is not in sight. China, Mugabe's current principal benefactor, is focused on slowing internal demand and seems less willing to invest in Zimbabwe than in the past. In August 2014, President Mugabe came back from a high-profile visit to China with few commitments from Beijing for additional aid or investment. Prior to the trip, some media reports indicated that Mugabe was hoping for commitments by China for as much as $4 billion in new funding.

The government's misguided economic policies, including land confiscation and forced "indigenization" of businesses, continue to have the predictable results of depressing productivity. According to the World Bank, Zimbabwe's gross domestic product (GDP) growth rate is falling and will decline to less than 1 percent annually by 2016. Difficult economic circumstances could lead to both civil unrest and new flows of refugees. The opposition MDC party, which was credited with the currency reform that ended the last economic emergency, might reemerge as a political force.

WARNING INDICATORS

The following developments could provide warning of likely instability in Zimbabwe:

- *Indications of Mugabe's declining health.* Mugabe remains remarkably vigorous, holding to a work and travel schedule that would challenge a person decades younger. Observers need to be alert to any changes in these patterns and the frequency of his appearances at official and ceremonial functions. Any evidence of diminished vigor on his part would be significant.

- *Signs of increasing dissent, infighting, and factionalism within the ZANU-PF.* The state and ruling party are inextricably intertwined. Mugabe's "guided democracy" has long been the decisive factor in resolving debates over party rules and offices. With his latest moves, however, Mugabe has taken his personal control to a new level. Significant opposition to Mugabe's authoritarian role would likely be met by repressive measures, but conceivably could trigger a crisis within the ZANU-PF.

- *Public unrest.* The security establishment, led by the "securocrats"—the senior leaders of the police and armed forces—controls not only the muscles of the state, but also a significant portion of the nation's economy. Civil violence or mass civil disobedience is unlikely as long as the grip of the securocrats remains firm. The failure of security forces to curb protests, strikes, and demonstrations through the use of force and intimidation might be an indicator of divisions among the securocrats. Observers should watch for changes in the major military and police commands and possible movements of army and police units. Likewise, it will be important to watch for increased willingness on the part of the political opposition and civil society groups to carry out protest activities.

IMPLICATIONS FOR U.S. INTERESTS

A serious political crisis in Zimbabwe could affect U.S. interests in several ways. It could generate a significant humanitarian problem that would likely require an expensive U.S. aid commitment. It could also delay hope of a productive bilateral trade and economic relationship, since U.S. trade with Zimbabwe would remain minimal. (In 2012, just over $50 million worth of goods and services flowed in each direction.) Bilateral political relations, trade, and investment would continue to be limited by legally mandated sanctions. A crisis could require U.S. military forces to evacuate the small U.S. citizen population in the country, estimated in 2010 at less than one thousand. Perhaps more important, a crisis in Zimbabwe could lead to potential friction with South Africa and other SADC member states on how to respond to human rights violations by the Zimbabwean government.

On the other hand, a stable and prosperous Zimbabwe would likely advance U.S. interests in Africa. Zimbabwe's rich endowment in human and natural resources would allow it to play a leading role in shaping Africa's future. Bilateral trade and investment would probably not increase rapidly, but would likely build over time. Revival of Zimbabwe's agricultural sector—perhaps with the benefit of American expertise—would obviate continued humanitarian food aid. Eventually, Zimbabwe's police and armed forces could be expected to play constructive roles in SADC and African Union peace operations. Zimbabwe would become a more attractive destination for U.S. tourists, resulting in improved interpersonal relations.

PREVENTIVE OPTIONS

In crafting a preventive strategy for Zimbabwe, it is important to acknowledge that the United States possesses few policy instruments for directly influencing developments. High-level bilateral meetings take place in Washington, in Harare, and at the United Nations, but the relationship is, at best, formal and official. President Mugabe continues to characterize the United States as a hostile force.

U.S. assistance to Zimbabwe is significant, totaling $130 million in 2013, but withdrawal of development assistance would have little effect on the policies of the government because aid is already channeled through civil society groups. The government in Harare quite likely assumes that U.S. humanitarian assistance would continue even if political repression increases. Targeted economic sanctions remain in place, but are widely seen as having little impact. Mugabe uses the sanctions as justification for promoting popular resentment toward the United States.

The United States could, broadly speaking, pursue two types of preventive strategies toward Zimbabwe. First, it could attempt to shape the outcome of the political transition though a combination of positive and negative incentives. The factors mentioned above, however, constrain the likelihood of this preventive strategy succeeding. Furthermore, the United States would have few, if any, partners in attempting to influence a succession in Zimbabwe. SADC, led by South Africa, has welcomed Mugabe back into its fold and is unlikely to reverse course. Beijing, which has great influence on the government in Harare, is not in the business of promoting democratic change. Even the European allies have begun limited economic partnerships with Zimbabwe and are unlikely to be willing to join in an activist strategy.

Second, the United States could accept the improbability of influencing the transition process and focus on minimizing the risk of political violence and economic turmoil, while also positioning itself to take advantage of post-succession opportunities to promote political and economic reform. This option would allow the succession drama within the ZANU-PF to run its course. A relatively swift and uncontested succession would enable the government of Zimbabwe to move past its political infighting and begin to attend to the economic and social challenges that the nation faces. This option would have much more modest goals than the first preventive option, aiming only to reduce the likelihood and potential severity of political violence and economic turmoil during the transition period.

Even though no single outside actor has the capacity to directly influence President Mugabe's choices regarding succession, a well-orchestrated multilateral strategy could help Mugabe and others in leadership positions understand the potential negative consequences of decisions that would increase repression, deepen the country's economic problems, and lead to social instability. In such a strategy, the United States would maintain its support for civil society in Zimbabwe and continue a frank and direct dialogue with the Mugabe government. Additionally, it would seek to persuade South Africa and the other SADC countries, China, and the European Union (EU) countries to act along the following lines.

South Africa and Zimbabwe's other SADC partners could, in the interest of regional stability, shed their usual reticence and remind President Mugabe of his responsibilities under the organization's statute to maintain peace and stability in his own country. Especially in the event that Mugabe might attempt to use his role as chair of SADC to justify repressive actions, it would be important for his SADC counterparts, especially South African President Jacob Zuma, to personally intervene. To the extent that Mugabe sees his SADC chairmanship as part of his legacy, he might be motivated to see his term through without controversy.

China is Zimbabwe's most important economic partner with bilateral trade of over $1 billion annually. Recently, China has refrained from large new investment commitments, perhaps over concerns for stability in Zimbabwe. In the interest of protecting its sizable investments in Zimbabwe, China might be motivated to quietly indicate to Mugabe its concerns over the possibility of instability.

The EU countries could increase their involvement with civil society organizations in Zimbabwe and indicate clearly to the Mugabe government that they would consider reimposing sanctions should greater repression of the opposition become the norm or should political violence break out.

MITIGATING OPTIONS

As efforts to prevent violence and instability in Zimbabwe move forward, the United States could act on a parallel track to reduce the consequences of any potential violence. It could coordinate preparatory measures with several international partners.

With South Africa and other SADC partners, there could be quiet, advance consultations regarding possible SADC actions in the event of violence in Zimbabwe. Possible SADC actions in the event of a crisis in Zimbabwe would include a prompt condemnation of violence and a call for opposing factions to lay down arms and cease provocative behavior. Although such a hortatory statement would have little direct effect, it would provide a foundation for eventual, more substantive measures such as the dispatch of a high-level mission to mediate among opposing factions in Zimbabwe. In addition, South Africa and other states bordering Zimbabwe could ensure that they are prepared to deal with additional refugees, should violence or an economic crisis prompt new emigration from Zimbabwe.

China would be unlikely to agree to consult in advance on actions that it might take in the event of violence in Zimbabwe. Nevertheless, Zimbabwe could be given a prominent place on the agenda for U.S.-Chinese consultations on Africa. Sharing information and reviewing the range of options available might increase the likelihood that China would use its influence with the government of Zimbabwe to prevent violence.

With the EU countries, the United States could coordinate contingency planning for humanitarian assistance, including food aid, both inside Zimbabwe and among populations of refugees outside the country. In addition, the United States and European countries could agree to form a contact group to track developments in Zimbabwe and prepare for advocating action by the UN Security Council to attempt to bring an end to political violence in Zimbabwe.

If, despite these efforts, significant political violence occurs in Zimbabwe, prompt action would be needed to prevent widespread loss of life and destruction of vital infrastructure. U.S. policy options include the following:

- *Intervention by SADC.* During the political and economic crisis that preceded the 2008 elections in Zimbabwe, SADC gave Thabo Mbeki, the former president of South Africa, a mandate to negotiate an accord between ZANU-PF and the two wings of the MDC. He successfully brokered an agreement, helping lower the level of preelection violence during the 2008 election campaign. Mbeki's effort could serve as a precedent for SADC in the event of renewed violence. The choice of mediator would be crucial. A South African would be most likely to gain Mugabe's attention and cooperation, but President Zuma seems preoccupied with internal challenges. Although not Mugabe's equal in rank, South African Vice President Cyril Ramaphosa has had recent mediation experience in Lesotho and would be an option.

- *Action by the UN Security Council.* Although the Security Council holds a mandate to act only with regard to threats to international peace and security, the latter concept has often been interpreted expansively. China might block decisive action by the Security Council, but might agree to the creation of a UN special envoy for Zimbabwe, including a mandate to contact all the internal parties in Zimbabwe with the objective of negotiating a ceasefire.

- *Coordinated increases in economic sanctions.* Broadening – sanctions would have a mainly symbolic effect. Reimposition of EU sanctions, however, would have a more powerful effect on the calculus of the Mugabe government.

- *Intensified official U.S. and Western dialogue with moderates in the ZANU-PF.* Many senior figures in the ZANU-PF have extensive business interests that would be damaged by prolonged civil unrest. Their interest in limiting violence might be a basis for dialogue.

- *Increased U.S. humanitarian assistance.* Additional humanitarian assistance, especially food aid, would be important both to saving lives and to countering the Mugabe government's demonization of the United States and the West. In past times of economic hardship, the Mugabe regime has threatened to block Western assistance, but has never made good on its bluster.

RECOMMENDATIONS

There is both time and opportunity for effective action to reduce the likelihood of political instability and civil violence in Zimbabwe, while also preparing for a transition to better governance and economic prosperity. In crafting its approach to a post-Mugabe Zimbabwe, the United States should think and plan ahead, with its broad regional interests in mind.

Even as its bilateral relationships with the governments of East and West Africa have grown stronger, the United States' ties with the SADC countries have tended to stagnate. This has been particularly true in the case of South Africa. While differences over Zimbabwe have not been the primary driver of U.S. relationships with the southern African region, they have been a significant negative element.

Yet, despite the uncertain political leadership of the Zuma government, labor unrest, and economic weaknesses, South Africa remains the most capable nation on the continent and an indispensable partner for the United States. In recent years, South Africa has begun to take a more active interest in African security issues, employing its armed forces as peacekeepers and its officials as peacemakers. Establishing a more active and constructive partnership in addressing African security challenges would benefit both countries.

Zimbabwe presents an opportunity to begin strengthening the partnership. The United States and South Africa share interests in promoting stability and peaceful change in Zimbabwe. South Africa would be the country most burdened by any new influx of refugees from Zimbabwe. Persistent economic depression in Zimbabwe damages the export economy of South Africa, which is Zimbabwe's largest trading partner. Although Zimbabwe weighs far less on U.S. interests, the risks and costs of a potential breakdown there are considerable. Bilateral U.S.–South African differences on Zimbabwe have been more over tone and tactics than over ultimate objectives, and better understanding and coordination should be within reach.

With these interests in mind, the United States should put in place a strategy for dealing with the threat of instability and civic violence in Zimbabwe. Early contacts with South Africa, other SADC countries, European allies, and China should be pursued. The U.S. policy agenda should include the following:

- *Intensify interagency efforts to define U.S. interests and options in Zimbabwe.* In the context of a formal interagency contingency planning effort on Zimbabwe, the U.S. government should assess the current situation, achieve consensus on the goal of limiting violence and economic turmoil in Zimbabwe, and define the incentives and disincentives available to influence the actions of the Mugabe government or its successor. Given the proven capacity of the government in Harare to bob, weave, and dissemble in the face of proffered incentives and disincentives, it would be wise to avoid aiming at a U.S. "roadmap" for Zimbabwe. Rather, the objective should be an integrated approach that would focus on practical, measurable steps that the government of Zimbabwe could take to permit a greater range of political expression and to liberalize the economy. Just as is the case with relations with other countries, the emphasis should be on changing actual practices rather than altering the radical rhetoric of the ZANU-PF.

- *Open a consultative channel on Zimbabwe with Congress.* Although Zimbabwe is far down the current list of executive branch foreign policy priorities with Congress, it is important to establish a consultative process with Congress in parallel to the interagency effort described above. Initially at least, these consultations should be at the staff level with the relevant subcommittees and with representatives of relevant members. The purpose of this channel would be to help members of Congress understand that positive change in Zimbabwe is likely to take place incrementally if at all to avoid confronting Congress with unpleasant surprises and to build a basis of trust for actions, whether carrots or sticks, further down the road.

- *Pursue understandings on Zimbabwe with South Africa and other SADC countries.* South Africa possesses the greatest potential influence on Zimbabwe's government and would also be directly affected by a crisis there. Conversations with the Zuma government should focus on achieving South African agreement to consistently urge President Mugabe and other ZANU-PF leaders to avoid violence. South Africa should also be prepared to mediate between factions in the ZANU-PF, as well as between ZANU-PF and the opposition, should widespread violence appear imminent.

- *Consult regularly on Zimbabwe with senior African affairs officials in EU countries.* These contacts should be made based on the results of U.S. interagency conclusions. The United States should aim to reach a common assessment of the situation and to work toward consensus on positive and negative incentives for Zimbabwe, including sanctions. There should also be agreement to coordinate public statements by Western governments in the event of a crisis in Zimbabwe.

- *Seek to influence China on Zimbabwe.* The United States currently consults with China on a variety of African issues, and China has begun to contribute to international efforts on the continent, including peace operations in South Sudan and antipiracy patrols off the coast of Somalia. Due to the potential consequences of a crisis in Zimbabwe for both

U.S. and Chinese interests, the United States should propose regular, in-depth conversations on Zimbabwe, focused on persuading the Chinese government to support a peaceful political transition in Zimbabwe.

- *Seek senior-level dialogue with the Zimbabwean government in multiple venues.* Contacts between the U.S. embassy in Harare and senior ZANU-PF figures are constrained by the tense relationship between the two capitals and party officials' fear of incurring Mugabe's wrath by appearing too close to American representatives. To supplement contacts by the embassy, the United States should seek to strengthen parallel communications channels in Washington and at the United Nations. Coordinated messaging in all three channels will be essential. The United States might seek to validate these channels by proposing small incentives, such as promoting greater U.S. investment in Zimbabwe in return for agreement by the Mugabe government to suspend aspects of its most objectionable economic policies, including "indigenization."

- *Expand youth and student exchanges.* Zimbabwe already participates in the U.S. government's Young African Leader Initiative (YALI). Consideration should be given to further expanding access by young Zimbabweans to YALI and similar programs. Although the objective effect of such a decision would not be immediate, it would be a timely counter to the argument of the Mugabe government that the United States has abandoned the people of Zimbabwe.

- *Ensure the security of the U.S. mission in Zimbabwe.* In the event of significant civil unrest, U.S. interests in Zimbabwe could become the target of violence. Plans for ensuring the security of the embassy and its personnel and for conducting an evacuation of those personnel if necessary should be updated regularly.

To encourage stability and prosperity in Zimbabwe beyond the transition, the United States should prioritize the following long-term recommendation:

- *Test the waters for expanding the bilateral dialogue.* Given the economic plight of Zimbabwe and its humanitarian needs, there is potential for cooperation with a new government on trade and commercial issues. Since the actual reach of sanctions has been less than that claimed by the Mugabe government, it would be possible to begin to unfreeze the bilateral relationship relatively easily with agreement on such steps as trade and investment missions. The United States should then pursue political dialogue in close coordination with its Western allies and South Africa. Keeping SADC in the lead publically while actively pursuing private diplomacy would probably increase the likelihood of measured, step-by-step progress.

CONCLUSION

Zimbabwe's problems, which have been created by decades of authoritarian misrule and poor economic management, will not be quickly solved. Any successor to Mugabe will have to deal with a bitter political legacy and difficult economic conditions. The alternatives open to the United States are limited by strained political relationships and minimal economic ties. This scarcity of options is not a rationale for doing little or nothing. Rather, it is a call for the United States to focus on what is essential—reducing the possibility of political instability and civil violence during the post-Mugabe succession—while laying the groundwork for a better relationship with an eventual successor government.

A VENEZUELAN REFUGEE CRISIS

Shannon K. O'Neil

Venezuela is in an economic free fall. As a result of government-led mismanagement and corruption, the currency value is plummeting, prices are hyperinflated, and gross domestic product (GDP) has fallen by over a third in the last five years. In an economy that produces little except oil, the government has cut imports by over 75 percent, choosing to use its hard currency to service the roughly $140 billion in debt and other obligations.

These economic choices have led to a humanitarian crisis. Basic food and medicines for Venezuela's approximately thirty million citizens are increasingly scarce, and the devastation of the health-care system has spurred outbreaks of treatable diseases and rising death rates. President Nicolas Maduro is pushing the nation toward authoritarianism, shutting down the free press, marginalizing the opposition-led legislature, barring opposition parties from participating in elections, and imprisoning political opponents, and in the summer of 2017 broke the democratic constitutional order with the illegitimate election of a constituent assembly.

The economic and humanitarian crises, combined with rising political persecution, have forced many Venezuelans to flee; around five hundred thousand have left the country in the last two years alone. If conditions worsen, many more Venezuelans could flow into neighboring countries. Colombia would be burdened the most by these outflows, given the length of the shared border, the commercial links, and

---

This Contingency Planning Memorandum was originally published in February 2018. See Shannon K. O'Neil, "A Venezuelan Refugee Crisis," Council on Foreign Relations, February 2018, http://cfr.org/report/venezuelan-refugee-crisis.

the personal ties millions of Venezuelans have there. Brazil, Guyana, and nearby Caribbean islands would also see an uptick in refugees that could overwhelm clinics and schools and potentially destabilize local economies and polities.

The United States should consider not only the potential damage and disruption caused to Venezuela's neighbors by a refugee crisis but also the implications of the crisis for U.S. interests. The economic, national security, and health costs imposed on the United States by a potential disruption in Venezuelan oil production, an increase in drug trafficking, or an epidemic, respectively, would be substantial. The United States can do little to prevent Venezuela's further downward spiral. However, it can and should take measures to mitigate the political, economic, and humanitarian consequences of a potential mass emigration.

THE CONTINGENCIES

Beginning with former President Hugo Chavez's ascent to power in 1999, an estimated two million Venezuelans have left their country. The outflow has escalated in recent months, with the majority of people crossing over to Colombia and Brazil; thousands of others have fled to nearby islands. According to the UN High Commissioner for Refugees (UNHCR), in 2016 twenty-seven thousand Venezuelans sought asylum worldwide; from January through July 2017 alone, more than fifty-two thousand applied for asylum. Over fifteen thousand of these have filed in the United States, making Venezuelans the most numerous asylum seekers in the country. Many times this number are departing Venezuela on other visa classifications and via informal routes. The UNHCR conservatively estimates that five thousand Venezuelans now reside in Curacao, twenty thousand in Aruba, thirty thousand in Brazil, forty thousand in Trinidad and Tobago, and over six hundred thousand in Colombia (see map).

These flows will likely continue, as Maduro's government remains unwilling to change economic direction. The possibility of these human outflows accelerating into mass emigration is also significant. Even if 5 percent of the current population fled (a smaller percentage than recent outflows from Syria or Yemen), that would mean well over one million migrants. And if the composition of the Venezuelan flows were similar to that of other refugee crises, half of those fleeing would be children.

Three circumstances could trigger this acceleration in outflows: a sharp deterioration in food supply, an epidemic, or an explosion of violence. Any of these three would further increase the likelihood of a refugee crisis.

Collapse of the Food Supply

An overwhelming majority of Venezuelans already lack easy access to food and daily necessities. Surveys report that nearly nine in ten Venezuelans have difficulty purchasing food; relatedly, three out of four Venezuelans have lost weight, an average of nineteen pounds just in 2017.

Years of intervention, nationalization, and expropriation have decimated local agriculture. The vast majority of food now comes from abroad, and distribution is firmly in the hands of the Maduro-aligned military. In addition to providing the food sold in price-controlled supermarkets and restaurants, the military directly distributes basic products to nearly six million families, roughly 70 percent of the population, through local provision and production committees (CLAPs). According to news reports, a good amount of this official food supply is sold on the black market. This control gives military officers—and their families—access to food as well as significant power and enrichment opportunities. Already there have been reports of uneven access to the military-distributed food packages through CLAPs. If the prevalence of food diminishes, whether at government-controlled prices or on the black market, desperate Venezuelans would flee in larger numbers.

The government increasingly needs to choose between using its hard currency to pay external debt obligations and feeding its population. In 2017, it chose to reduce food and other essential imports by nearly 30 percent in order to meet debt payments of $10 billion. The government owes another $10 billion in 2018 and $14 billion in 2019. U.S. financial sanctions have made it virtually impossible to roll over or raise new money in international markets, and Russian and Chinese loans have not covered the shortfalls. If the government chooses to continue servicing its obligations, food insecurity could worsen to an extent that drives mass emigration.

Inflationary pressures could also cause a collapse in the food supply. With the International Monetary Fund (IMF) predicting inflation rates of over 2,000 percent in 2018, provisions on the black market could become out of reach for the average Venezuelan.

The consequences of a debt default are not wholly certain, but a default could further limit access to food. On the surface, a default would free public money for food and medicine by lowering or ending external debt servicing. Additionally, the ensuing economic chaos could lead to regime change and new economic policies that could alleviate the current hardships and migration pressures. However, if the current government remained in power, so too would U.S. financial sanctions. That would make an IMF stabilization package and a broader debt restructuring impossible in the event of a default, further limiting access to hard currency and imports. The ensuing economic dislocations could disrupt food distribution to segments of the population.

Given the politicization of access to food, rising political opposition—combined with increasing restrictions on financial resources for any of the reasons above—could push the government to intentionally starve opposition-controlled areas, forcing many to leave.

Outbreak of Disease

Access to basic health care has declined precipitously in Venezuela. One-fifth of the country's medical personnel have fled the country in the past four years alone. Understaffed hospitals are also underequipped: over half lack enough beds for patients, three out of four are missing the basic drugs on the World Health Organization (WHO) list of essential medicines, and two out of five are without drinkable water.

The health-care system is incapable of dealing with rising child malnutrition, which now exceeds the WHO's crisis threshold, according to Caritas, a Catholic charity. A 2015 Ministry of Health report reveals that over 2 percent of all newborns die in their first four weeks, up from 0.02 percent three years ago. The maternal mortality rate has increased nearly fivefold in the same period.

With the collapse of basic health infrastructure, treatable and communicable diseases have spread. Diabetes and hypertension have doubled in the last year. Deaths from HIV/AIDS are ascending rapidly in Venezuela—once a model for HIV/AIDS management—even as they decline regionally, as more than one hundred thousand Venezuelans living with HIV/AIDS have no access to medication. Several outbreaks of tuberculosis, diphtheria, and Chagas disease have been reported among an increasingly malnourished population. A former health minister estimates that over half a million Venezuelans have contracted malaria. Vaccines have largely disappeared, leaving at least one million children vulnerable to measles. An epidemic of one of these or other deadlier diseases could cause a mass emigration, particularly from urban centers. Refugees would likely carry the illness to neighboring countries and strain the already overcrowded border hospitals.

Venezuelans face persistent insecurity in their daily lives. Homicides in Caracas top 140 per 100,000 people, far outpacing rates in Baghdad and Kabul. Almost 40 percent of Venezuelans report having been robbed in the last year. A newer phenomenon of politically oriented violence has been on the rise. During street protests in 2017, more than 150 Venezuelans were killed by government forces, mainly the National Guard. If politically motivated violence escalates, it could lead to mass emigration. Such violence could be spurred by divisions within the opposition or the regime.

In response to the authoritarian moves of the Maduro government, the political opposition has worked to find democratic avenues for change. These have included contesting and winning a two-thirds majority in the legislature in 2015 (only to have the Maduro-controlled Supreme Court annul nearly all of its legislation), pushing for a constitutionally allowed presidential-recall referendum (stymied again by the politicized court system), protesting the illegitimate constituent assembly election process, and more recently participating in—and losing—manipulated regional elections.

With few legal avenues now available, the political opposition has fragmented, opening space for more radical elements within to turn to more violent tactics and potentially to arms. If this occurs, the government would likely respond swiftly and harshly, leading to hundreds if not thousands of deaths and potentially forcing opposition members and sympathizers to flee.

Discord is also reported among the United Socialist Party of Venezuela (PSUV) members and supporters, some of whom allege that Maduro has betrayed Chavez's ideals in word and deed by overturning his 1999 constitution. Several high- and middle-ranking military officers have also been arrested, allegedly for plotting coups.

Further schisms, particularly among or within the four main security forces—the military, the National Guard, government-controlled militias, and neighborhood vigilante groups called *colectivos*—could lead to an explosion of civil unrest and even fighting in the streets. It could also lead to generalized disorder and more impunity. Any of these scenarios could cause citizens to flee.

A majority of refugees would likely flee to Colombia given geographic, commercial, and familial ties. Every day, about twenty-five thousand Venezuelans cross the 1,378-mile-long border to buy basic goods—adding up to over nine million visits a year. As the situation worsens, some of them could decide to stay in Colombia. In addition, over five million people of Colombian origin live in Venezuela, many of whom had been displaced in the 1980s and 1990s by the violence caused by the Revolutionary Armed Forces of Colombia (FARC) and the paramilitary. If these Venezuelans chose to leave en masse, Colombia would be hard-pressed not to take them back.

Brazil too would be a major destination; desperate Venezuelans already account for the majority of hospital visits along the border. Tens—if not hundreds—of thousands could trek south on the sparse road system through the Amazon. Such a movement of people would undoubtedly strain the public resources of border states Roraima and Amazonas in Brazil, which has dealt with similarly sized refugee flows before, including from Haiti.

Additional possible destinations include Guyana and the nearby Caribbean islands of Antigua and Barbuda, Aruba, Curacao, and Trinidad and Tobago, which can absorb far fewer refugees. An influx of several thousand people could overwhelm local health, education, and basic shelter in nations already battered by hurricanes.

WARNING INDICATORS

Deteriorating economic and health measures and increased political persecution and violence could accelerate refugee flows. Further steep declines in GDP, oil revenues, or foreign currency reserves along with sharp increases in inflation and unemployment would signal toughening circumstances for individuals and families. As the combination of hyperinflation and the government's inability to print enough new bills undermines the use of currency, scarcity and hardship would intensify. In terms of health, rapidly rising maternal mortality rates have already led to mass flows of pregnant women to hospitals across the borders. Reports of new disease outbreaks or fast-rising death tolls would suggest a spreading epidemic that could begin to drive greater population movements. Street protests and government repression escalated from April to July 2017, leaving over 150 people dead, 2,000 injured, and 5,400 incarcerated. Since then, demonstrations have faded. Another uptick met with a heavy-handed response could spur the movement of people. So too could exhortations by Maduro for vigilante justice against his opponents or explicit exclusion of opposition sympathizers from accessing publicly provided food and basic services. Other political warning indicators include an increase in politically motivated violence or assassinations and the formation of armed groups.

Another set of warning indicators would include countries becoming more open to receiving Venezuelans so that the costs of leaving are lowered. Recent steps include Colombia granting temporary legal status to more than 150,000 Venezuelans who overstayed visas, Peru introducing a special visa to allow Venezuelans already in the country to study and work for a year, and Argentina making it easier for Venezuelans to obtain a work permit.

IMPLICATIONS FOR U.S. INTERESTS

Massive human outflows from Venezuela could destabilize the politics, economics, and security of neighboring nations and thus significantly harm U.S. national security interests. These challenges come at a particularly delicate time for Colombia, as the longtime U.S. ally works to implement a historic peace process with former FARC guerrillas. An influx of refugees into formerly FARC-controlled border communities could undermine stabilization efforts by imposing an added economic and humanitarian burden on local authorities. Also threatened are the small Caribbean islands, where even a few thousand migrants could overwhelm local services and increase social tensions. Many of these countries lack legal frameworks and departments to process asylum seekers and migrants, further complicating matters.

A refugee crisis could hinder U.S. efforts to defeat transnational drug and criminal organizations. Venezuela has become a major transit country for Colombian cocaine headed to the United States and Europe, with reported involvement of high-ranking officials in drug trafficking and organized crime. (President Donald J. Trump has publicly criticized Colombia's failure to crack down on coca production, which surged to a decade high in 2017; about 90 percent of cocaine in the United States comes from Colombia.) A refugee wave could aggravate these challenges, as criminal organizations could abuse a large and vulnerable population for recruitment or as prey for human trafficking.

In the event of an epidemic, mass migration would be accompanied by a health crisis across the Americas, including in the United States.

Turmoil within Venezuela could also disrupt the daily flow of the seven hundred thousand barrels of Venezuelan oil to U.S. refineries—roughly 8 percent of all oil imports—hampering individual businesses in Louisiana, Mississippi, and Texas and likely raising retail gas rates by twenty to thirty cents a gallon.

President Trump has spoken consistently on the need for democracy and humanitarian assistance in Venezuela, personally met members of the Venezuelan opposition, and discussed Venezuela during his meetings with Latin American heads of state. The U.S. State Department has called on the Venezuelan government to allow international aid into the country; in UN Security Council meetings, Ambassador Nikki Haley has reaffirmed the United States' humanitarian commitment to Venezuela. Tens of thousands of Venezuelan Americans and over two hundred thousand Colombian Americans reside in the swing state of Florida; this domestic electoral incentive drives broad congressional support for a restoration of democracy in Venezuela and the provision of humanitarian aid to the country.

PREVENTIVE OPTIONS

To prevent a refugee crisis across the Americas, the United States, other nations, and multilateral organizations could pursue policies designed to encourage Venezuelans to stay in their homes rather than flee. As these contingency scenarios result from the Maduro government's economic mismanagement, widespread corruption, and repressive tendencies, Venezuela needs to change its economic, political, and social policies to keep its citizens home. This requires a change in government and likely a restoration of democracy.

The United States, other nations, and international organizations have already tried a mix of diplomacy and sanctions to expand the governing coalition and force a transition. A 2016 initiative led by former Dominican, Panamanian, and Spanish leaders and supported by Pope Francis failed after the Venezuelan government refused to meet its initial commitments, including freeing political prisoners and setting an electoral timetable. The European Union (EU) could not generate enough pressure to restart a dialogue in September 2017. In December 2017, members of the opposition, along with civil society organizations, returned to negotiations with government representatives in the Dominican Republic, with Bolivia, Chile, Mexico, and Nicaragua acting as guarantors. No agreement has yet been reached yet.

The Organization of American States (OAS) has attempted to name and shame the Venezuelan government into changing its political behavior, but it has been unable to amass the two-thirds majority necessary to suspend Venezuela from the organization. The OAS is now working to bring members of the Maduro government to the International Criminal Court for crimes against humanity, including political and human rights abuses against the opposition. A group of twelve countries—including Argentina, Brazil, Canada, and Mexico—has also formed to condemn Venezuela's undemocratic practices.

Within the United Nations, several member states and bodies, including the UN Human Rights Council, have identified human rights violations in Venezuela and called for investigations into crimes against humanity. At the Security Council, however, veto holders China and Russia have prevented concrete initiatives against the regime. Efforts made so far have failed to change the actions of the Maduro government in ways that would alleviate human suffering and stop the flow of migrants.

Sanctions represent another means of pressure. The Barack Obama and Donald Trump administrations have cumulatively sanctioned over forty Venezuelan individuals for human rights abuses or support of terrorist and drug trafficking organizations by freezing their assets, restricting access to the U.S. financial system, banning them from the United States, and forbidding them from doing business with U.S. citizens. In August 2017, the Trump administration levied financial sanctions on the Venezuelan government and the state-owned oil and gas company Petroleos de Venezuela, SA (PDVSA), limiting their access to U.S. financial markets and their ability to remit or even service outstanding debt obligations. Canada and the EU have also sanctioned corrupt Venezuelan individuals, and the EU has banned the sale of goods to Venezuela that could be used for repression.

The United States could intensify sanctions. It could expand the list of targeted individuals and ban the sale of the lighter U.S. crude oil and diluents that Venezuela needs to pump its heavy crude and process it for export. This would temporarily disrupt production, as the Maduro government looks for other sources. The United States could also refuse to pay PDVSA directly for oil shipped to U.S. refineries and instead set up an account that would only allow the purchase of food and medicines, along the lines of the United Nations' oil-for-food program in Iraq but this time with more stringent oversight. On the financial side, the United States could impose secondary sanctions on foreign entities that conduct business with Venezuela; these secondary sanctions would be similar to those levied on European banks that evaded sanctions on Iran or those that the United States threatened to impose on Chinese institutions handling North Korean-linked funds. Lastly, the United States could impose a full embargo on Venezuela's oil and petroleum products or on its economy as a whole, much like the Cuban embargo.

These actions could cause further hardship for Venezuelans if the regime does not fall quickly (which has been the experience with other sanctioned regimes), resulting in more refugees. Moreover, polls show that sanctions are unpopular even among Venezuelans who support the opposition; therefore, outside economic pressure risks increasing over-all sympathy for the regime rather than weakening its political hold.

A major impediment to the success of these diplomatic and eco-nomic policy options is the criminal history of many Venezuelan government officials. The top echelon includes individuals already sanctioned by the United States for human rights abuses, corruption, and undemocratic practices. Sealed indictments allegedly detail Vene-zuelan officials' roles in drug trafficking and extensive corruption. For these officials, a democratic transition would likely mean incarceration; this possibility hardens their resolve to remain in power.

Military action, which the Trump administration has floated as a possibility, is inappropriate for this situation. The concrete objectives for such action remain vague, and significant resources would be neces-sary to occupy the nation for what could be an extended period of time.

While a military option could begin with air and other limited strikes, the significant possibility of a government collapse and ensuing civil war would require preparation for a full-blown invasion and occu-pation. Venezuela is double the size of Iraq; to secure it, the U.S. military would need to plan for the presence of 150,000 or more troops. Much as in Iraq, these forces would likely need to remain not only to oversee new elections but also to enable a democratically elected government to regain control of portions of the country, to maintain stability, and potentially to rebuild physical and other infrastructure. A Venezuelan presence would draw attention and resources away from other security threats around the globe.

Polls show a majority of Venezuelans, and a plurality of opposition supporters, are against current U.S. financial sanctions. A military intervention would be even less popular. U.S. troops would be greeted, at least by a significant segment of the population, as oppressors.

The United States would also face staunch opposition from other Latin American nations, which roundly condemned President Trump's suggestion of a military option last year. While a number of Latin Amer-ican nations might be convinced to join the United States, Canada, and the European Union in sanctioning individual Venezuelan leaders for human rights, corruption, and other abuses (they have yet to do so), any military involvement or action by Venezuela's neighbors, whether with the United States or on their own, would run counter to over one hundred years of Latin America's nonintervention foreign policy consensus as well as go against the wishes of their voting publics.

Latin American nations have been able and willing to send troops to participate in UN peacekeeping operations, including regional missions in Guatemala and Haiti. Such a mandate is unlikely in Venezuela due to China's and Russia's ties to the Maduro government. If the current regime ended and the United Nations authorized such an effort, Latin American nations would likely join. A change in regime would also likely bring a change in economic policy, alleviating other pressures to migrate.

As it stands, the near consensus condemning the Maduro regime today would likely turn toward the United States if it intervened militarily. And the increased instability and violence resulting from an intervention could heighten a refugee crisis, leading more Venezuelans to flee.

Another way to persuade people to remain in Venezuela is by making their lives there more bearable, mainly through humanitarian assistance. This step would require the consent of the Maduro regime, which despite numerous offers has not allowed aid to enter the country. It would also be difficult to keep the Venezuelan government from controlling and using the aid to bolster its power.

Finally, the United States could work with neighboring countries to close their borders, making it harder for Venezuelans to flee. But this option is anti-humanitarian. It is also impractical given that hundreds of miles of border remain unguarded and that most Venezuelans currently fleeing are not going through formal application processes. Moreover, it would be politically difficult for the Colombian government to deny entry to over five million Venezuelans of Colombian origin, many of whom left Colombia in the 1980s and 1990s due to drug-related violence.

Overall, the United States has few effective preventive tools or strategies to compel the change in Venezuela's policy or government needed to alleviate the current suffering. Therefore, the United States should focus its efforts on mitigating the detrimental effects on those fleeing and on their recipient countries.

MITIGATING OPTIONS

The United States could help Venezuela's neighbors mitigate a refugee crisis by creating a U.S. interagency refugee plan as the basis for a larger coordination effort. The U.S. Agency for International Development (USAID) in conjunction with the State Department's Bureau of Population, Refugees, and Migration (PRM) and the Defense Department's

Southern Command could prepare a refugee policy—one that builds on lessons learned in Syria and South Sudan—to be implemented largely by nongovernmental and multilateral organizations working in the region.

In addition to coordinating among the agencies, U.S. officials could create multilateral or multinational refugee plans, whereby the U.S. government would work with other organizations or governments to provide monetary, personnel, or supply assistance to refugees. On the ground, this assistance could contribute to expanding intake centers and building shelters, clinics, schools, warehouses, and other humanitarian infrastructure for the delivery of basic goods and services for families. Assistance could also take the form of transportation funds for Venezuelans fleeing to other, less burdened nations.

The United States could push the World Bank and the Inter-American Development Bank (IADB), as the largest shareholder in both, to provide low-interest loans to middle-income countries (including Colombia and Brazil) to build infrastructure for refugees. The United States and partners, such as the EU or Japan, could guarantee these loans and fast-track the approval process.

More systematically, the United States could help countries that take in Venezuelans to develop asylum and refugee policies. The United States could encourage Guyana to sign the 1951 Refugee Convention and/or its 1967 protocol, thereby committing to accept and protect refugees. The United States could assist other Latin American nations that are already signatories (with the exception of Cuba) in developing refugee policies. It could also support refugee assistance efforts in these countries—as it has done in Lebanon for Syrian refugees—by funding food and shelter provisions, infrastructure projects, and the work of nongovernmental organizations (NGOs). Countries expecting or experiencing significant refugee inflows could work with multilateral agencies too, particularly the UNHCR, which can set up local offices to help in capacity building, support the development of an effective asylum system, and provide direct assistance to refugees and asylum seekers through and in coordination with local donors and NGOs.

The United States could spearhead the development of a broader burden-sharing arrangement, coordinating efforts across the region and with other allies around the world to alleviate the crisis both for those fleeing and for people in the refugee destinations. The United States could work with the EU and other donor nations to help recipient countries build social services and support for asylum-seeking and refugee families that may not be able to return to Venezuela for years.

RECOMMENDATIONS

Despite the limited chances for success, the United States should continue to pressure the Venezuelan government, preferably as part of a multinational coalition, for policy and political change. This means supporting diplomatic efforts and negotiations, despite the failure of previous efforts to bring about the desired outcomes.

In addition, the United States should increase legal and financial pressures on regime wrongdoers. While sectoral or economy-wide sanctions would likely aggravate the situation, individual sanctions limit the ability of transgressors and their families to enjoy their ill-gotten gains around the world. The Department of Justice should aggressively prosecute those who have committed crimes, including drug trafficking, money laundering, international fraud, and racketeering, while the Department of the Treasury should work with other countries to replicate existing U.S. sanctions on individuals.

Recognizing the difficulty in shaping events within Venezuela, the United States should concentrate on working with its allies in Venezuela's neighborhood and the region to ease the suffering of the refugees themselves as well as to mitigate the potential political, economic, and social disturbance in receiving nations. This involves creating a broader burden-sharing arrangement for processing refugees, providing immediate humanitarian aid, and helping build the necessary infrastructure to integrate potentially over a million individuals with families into new homes and countries. The United States should weave together a domestic interagency plan and an international effort focused on countries of first asylum, supported by nations and multilateral institutions both regional and global.

Internally, the State Department's PRM and the USAID Offices of Food for Peace (FFP) and Foreign Disaster Assistance (OFDA) should lead this effort, coordinating closely on logistics with the Southern Command given that Venezuela lies within its area of responsibility. Together they should work with regional and donor countries, and with multilateral agencies. With previous financial assistance for the internally displaced in Colombia and recent support for refugees in Yemen as guides, costs would range between $150 million and $200 million. Initiatives would include

- FFP coordinating with NGOs and the UN World Food Program to ensure rapid emergency food assistance;

- PRM and OFDA working with the International Committee of the Red Cross (ICRC) and UNHCR to create shelters and settlements;

- PRM working with the UN Children's Fund (UNICEF) to coordinate child protection; education; health; and water, sanitation, and hygiene;

- PRM working with the International Organization for Migration (IOM) and UNHCR to provide transportation, health, and essential survival items such as water containers, hygiene kits, blankets, and rechargeable lights;

- PRM working with ICRC, UNICEF, IOM, and WHO to provide medicine and surgical supplies;

- PRM working with NGOs to provide legal services and education; and

- PRM and the Treasury Department working with the IADB and the World Bank to provide infrastructure loans to Colombia and Brazil.

Following the Cuban example, the Maduro government is already encouraging migration as a way to diminish internal opposition—a trend likely to continue, if not escalate, in the months to come. These recommendations, if implemented, would serve to alleviate the pressure of a mass migration on Venezuela's neighbors, protect those fleeing, and lessen the risk of an epidemic or armed conflict and violence spreading more broadly. By making the region more secure and politically stable, even as it faces a potential refugee crisis, these policies will protect U.S. interests.

ENDNOTES

PREPARING FOR THE NEXT FOREIGN POLICY CRISIS:
WHAT THE UNITED STATES SHOULD DO

1. There is no generally accepted definition of a foreign policy or national security crisis, though there is broad consensus that such events have three common characteristics, namely that (1) they derive from an event or series of events perceived to be threatening to core national interests or values; (2) there is a sense of urgency to respond because of the perceived velocity of the threatening development, the estimated time required to execute a response, or the presence of a discrete deadline; and (3) decisions are taken amid significant uncertainty about the nature of the threat, what to do in response, or what the consequences (costs and benefits) might be. Some definitions have also stipulated that there be an element of surprise, but this is not considered a necessary condition. For a useful distillation of how the definition of a crisis in international relations has evolved, see Eric K. Stern, "Crisis Studies and Foreign Policy Analysis: Insights, Synergies, and Challenges," *International Studies Review* 5, no. 2 (June 2003): 183–202, http://doi.org/10.1111/1521-9488.5020016. See also Arjen Boin, Paul 't Hart, Eric Stern, and Bengt Sundelius, *The Politics of Crisis Management: Public Leadership Under Pressure*, 2nd ed. (Cambridge: Cambridge University Press, 2017).

2. The Council on Foreign Relations' Center for Preventive Action (CPA) list runs to October 2019, but because CPA relied on publicly available press releases and unclassified reports to determine whether an event merited inclusion in the list of crises included in the chapter "U.S. Foreign Policy Crises, 1989–2019," the final list of cases may not include more recent or still-classified events. See pages 18–23 in this report for a detailed explanation of methodology.

3. Many experts believe, for example, that had President George H.W. Bush taken more forceful action when Yugoslavia started to unravel and descend into civil war during the spring and summer of 1992, the subsequent bloodshed in the Balkans—and the eventual U.S. military intervention—could have been avoided. Similarly, it is now generally accepted that President Bill Clinton could have done more to stop the 1994 Rwandan genocide when the scope of the atrocities became apparent. Less clear, but nevertheless asserted by some experts, is the conviction that a more robust response

by President George W. Bush to Russia's 2008 intervention in Georgia would have deterred Russia's later interference in eastern Ukraine and annexation of Crimea. Likewise, it has become almost conventional wisdom that President Barack Obama erred in 2013 by not following through on his earlier red line threat to punish Syria for the use of chemical weapons. Many commentators have argued that Obama's inaction emboldened the Bashar al-Assad regime and its principal allies, Iran and Russia, to act more aggressively, causing the conflict to become even more violent and destabilizing. For examples, see Michael Dobbs, "A War That Could Have Been Prevented," *Foreign Policy*, May 9, 2012, http://foreignpolicy.com/2012/05/09/a-war-that-could-have -been-prevented; Colum Lynch, "Rwanda Revisited," *Foreign Policy*, April 5, 2015, http://foreignpolicy.com/2015/04/05/rwanda-revisited-genocide-united-states-state -department; Damien Sharkov, "Ukraine Blames International Response to Georgia Crisis for Russian Intervention," *Newsweek*, August 9, 2016, http://newsweek.com /ukraine-blames-un-international-response-georgia-crisis-russian-intervention-488734; and Derek Chollet, "Obama's Red Line, Revisited," *Politico Magazine*, July 19, 2016, http://politico.com/magazine/story/2016/07/obama-syria-foreign-policy-red-line -revisited-214059.

4. See, for example, Richard N. Haass, *A World in Disarray: American Foreign Policy and the Crisis of the Old Order* (New York: Penguin Press, 2016) and Robert Kagan, *The Jungle Grows Back: America and Our Imperiled World* (New York: Alfred A. Knopf, 2018).

5. See, for example, Ivo H. Daalder and James M. Lindsay, *The Empty Throne: America's Abdication of Global Leadership* (New York: Public Affairs, 2018).

6. See Charles Baubion, "OECD Risk Management: Strategic Crisis Management," OECD Working Paper on Public Governance, no. 23, 7, http://doi.org/10.1787 /5k41rbd1lzr7-en; and Seth D. Kaplan, "Risk Cascades and How to Manage Them," *American Interest*, March/April 2017, 101–109.

7. The seizure of U.S. merchant ships by French privateers between 1798 and 1800, followed by similar attacks against U.S. ships in the Mediterranean by Barbary pirates— which led to the First Barbary War from 1801 to 1805—were the first foreign policy crises that the United States faced.

8. See Barry R. Posen, *Restraint: A New Foundation for U.S. Grand Strategy* (Ithaca, NY: Cornell University Press, 2014); and Stephen M. Walt, *The Hell of Good Intentions: America's Foreign Policy Elite and the Decline of U.S. Primacy* (New York: Farrar, Straus and Giroux, 2018).

9. For a critique of what is often referred to as offshore balancing, see Hal Brands and Peter Feaver, "Should America Retrench? The Battle Over Offshore Balancing," *Foreign Affairs*, November/December 2016, http://foreignaffairs.com/articles/should -america-retrench; and Frank G. Hoffman, "Retreating Ashore: The Flaws of Offshore Balancing," *Geopoliticus* (blog), Foreign Policy Research Institute, July 5, 2016, http:// fpri.org/2016/07/retreating-ashore-flaws-offshore-balancing.

10. This was certainly the case for the first term of the Richard M. Nixon administration; see David Rothkopf, *Running the World: The Inside Story of the National Security Council and the Architects of American Power* (New York: Public Affairs, 2005), 118. For examples from the first term of the Bill Clinton administration, see Warren Christopher, *In the Stream of History: Shaping Foreign Policy for a New Era* (Stanford, CA: Stanford

University Press, 1998); and for examples from the first term of the Barack Obama administration, see Paul B. Stares and Micah Zenko, *Enhancing U.S. Preventive Action* (New York: Council on Foreign Relations, 2007), 3, http://cfr.org/report/enhancing -us-preventive-action.

11. Stares and Zenko, *Enhancing U.S. Preventive Action*, 8–9.

12. Paul B. Stares, "Enhancing U.S. Crisis Preparedness," Council on Foreign Relations, June 21, 2011, http://cfr.org/report/enhancing-us-crisis-preparedness.

13. Stares, "Enhancing U.S. Crisis Preparedness."

14. Stares, "Enhancing U.S. Crisis Preparedness."

15. See Philip Zelikow, "Smaller but Sharper," Miller Center, University of Virginia, January 14, 2016, http://millercenter.org/issues-policy/governance/smaller-but -sharper.

16. Stares, "Enhancing U.S. Crisis Preparedness."

17. To its credit, the U.S. Agency for International Development (USAID) does produce regular field manuals and technical briefs that provide practical guidance for its personnel.

18. William J. Burns, *The Back Channel: A Memoir of American Diplomacy and the Case for Its Renewal* (New York: Random House, 2019), 86. See also Charles A. Ray, "America Needs a Professional Foreign Service," *Foreign Service Journal* (July/August 2015), http://afsa.org/america-needs-professional-foreign-service.

19. Stares, "Enhancing U.S. Crisis Preparedness."

20. Stares and Zenko, *Enhancing U.S. Preventive Action*, 7–8. For a more thorough discussion and refinement of this approach, see Paul B. Stares, *Preventive Engagement: How America Can Avoid War, Stay Strong, and Keep the Peace* (New York: Columbia University Press, 2017), 66–89.

21. This, in essence, is the purpose of professional checklists for complex tasks. For further discussion of this technique, see Atul Gawande, *The Checklist Manifesto: How to Get Things Right* (New York: Picador, 2009). Interestingly, at the outset of his tenure as secretary of state, Dean Rusk advocated for much the same approach in a speech to his staff: "There is one type of study I have not seen, which I hope we can do something about in the months ahead. The pilot of a jet aircraft has a checklist of many dozen questions which he must answer satisfactorily before he takes his plane off on a flight. Would it not be interesting and revealing if we had a checklist of questions which we should answer systematically before we take off on a policy?" See "Dean Rusk, The Formulation of Foreign Policy (1961)," in *American Foreign Policy: Current Documents* (Washington, DC: U.S. Government Printing Office, 1961), 5.

22. See Stares, *Preventive Engagement*, 31–34.

23. For examples of other foresight techniques, see Stares, *Preventive Engagement*, 42–48.

24. The Pentagon's principal war planning document, *The Guidance for Employment of the Force (GEF)*, is a Title 10 requirement of the U.S. Code.

25. Steven Pifer, "Crisis Between Ukraine and Russia," Council on Foreign Relations, June 2009, http://cfr.org/report/crisis-between-ukraine-and-russia.

26. Steven A. Cook, "Political Instability in Egypt," Council on Foreign Relations, August 2009, http://cfr.org/report/political-instability-egypt.

27. Paul B. Stares, "Military Escalation in Korea," Council on Foreign Relations, November 2010, http://cfr.org/report/military-escalation-korea.

28. Daniel P. Serwer, "Post-Qaddafi Instability in Libya," Council on Foreign Relations, August 2011, http://cfr.org/report/post-qaddafi-instability-libya.

29. Daniel P. Serwer, "Libya's Escalating Civil War," Council on Foreign Relations, June 2015, http://cfr.org/report/libyas-escalating-civil-war.

30. Bonnie S. Glaser, "Armed Clash in the South China Sea," Council on Foreign Relations, April 2012, http://cfr.org/report/armed-clash-south-china-sea.

31. Bonnie S. Glaser, "Conflict in the South China Sea," Council on Foreign Relations, April 2015, http://cfr.org/report/conflict-south-china-sea.

32. Patrick Duddy, "Political Unrest in Venezuela," Council on Foreign Relations, September 2012, http://cfr.org/report/political-unrest-venezuela.

33. Patrick Duddy, "Political Crisis in Venezuela."

34. Daniel S. Markey, "Armed Confrontation Between China and India," Council on Foreign Relations, November 2015, http://cfr.org/report/armed-confrontation -between-china-and-india.

35. Seth G. Jones, "Strategic Reversal in Afghanistan," Council on Foreign Relations, June 2016, http://cfr.org/report/strategic-reversal-afghanistan.

36. One of the best arguments for this approach was formulated in a March 1969 national security decision memorandum that states: "It is recognized that not all contingencies can be anticipated and that the specifics of a particular anticipated contingency cannot be accurately predicted. Nevertheless, there are important advantages which might accrue from contingency planning, among which are: a clearer assessment of U.S. interests and possible need for U.S. action in a particular situation; an increased likelihood that U.S. actions taken will be timely and will minimize risks or losses; the possible discovery of actions which might resolve or head off a crisis; and the familiarization of key officials with factual material and alternative courses of action in event of a crisis." See National Security Council, "National Security Decision Memorandum 8: Crisis Anticipation and Management" (Washington, DC, March 1969).

37. See Gregory Treverton, "From Afghanistan to Trump: 2014–2017," in *Truth to Power: A History of the U.S. National Intelligence Council*, eds. Robert Hutchings and Gregory F. Treverton (New York: Oxford University Press, 2019), 191–193.

38. See Eric K. Stern, ed., *Designing Crisis Management Training and Exercises for Strategic Leaders*, Crismart 42, Swedish National Defense College, 2014.

39. For more, see Stares, *Preventive Engagement*, 223–244.

U.S. FOREIGN POLICY CRISES, 1989–2019

1. For the International Crisis Behavior project, see Michael Brecher and Jonathan

Wilkenfeld, *A Study of Crisis* (Ann Arbor: University of Michigan Press, 2000); see also Michael Brecher, Jonathan Wilkenfeld, Kyle Beardsley, Patrick James, and David Quinn, International Crisis Behavior Data Codebook, version 12 (2017), http://sites.duke.edu /icbdata/data-collections. For the Correlates of War project, see Meredith Reid Sarkees and Frank Wayman, *Resort to War: 1816–2007* (Washington, DC: CQ Press, 2010), http://correlatesofwar.org/data-sets/COW-war. For the Political Instability Task Force, see Political Instability Task Force (PITF), *Consolidated Problem Set, Historical State Armed Conflicts and Regime Crises, 1955–2017* (Vienna, VA: Center for Systemic Peace, 2017), http://systemicpeace.org/inscr/PITF%20Consolidated%20Case%20List %202017.pdf. For reports from the Congressional Research Service, see Barbara Salazar Torreon and Sofia Plagakis, "Instances of Use of United States Armed Forces Abroad, 1798–2019" (Washington, DC: Congressional Research Service, 2019), https://fas.org/sgp/crs/natsec/R42738.pdf. For the RAND Corporation report, see Jennifer Kavanaugh, Bryan Frederick, Alexandra Stark, Nathan Chandler, Meagan L. Smith, Matthew Povlock, Lynn E. Davis, and Edward Geist, *Characteristics of Successful U.S. Military Interventions* (Santa Monica, CA: RAND Corporation, 2019), 303–308, http://rand.org/pubs/research_reports/RR3062.html.

2. See, for example, the Global Terrorism Database: National Consortium for the Study of Terrorism and Responses to Terrorism (START) project at the University of Maryland (2018), available at http://start.umd.edu/gtd. See also the RAND Database of Worldwide Terrorism Incidents, available at http://rand.org/nsrd/projects/terrorism -incidents/download.html.

ACKNOWLEDGMENTS

Many people deserve to be thanked for their contributions to this compilation. Richard N. Haass, president of the Council on Foreign Relations, as well as Senior Vice President and Director of Studies James M. Lindsay and Vice President and Deputy Director of Studies Shannon K. O'Neil merit special mention not only for their support of the work of the Center for Preventive Action, but also for their substantive help in bringing to fruition many of the publications that this report draws upon.

I am also grateful for the guidance and support of Patricia Dorff and her terrific team of editors over the years, particularly Julie Hersh and Sumit Poudyal. I have been extremely fortunate, moreover, to work with a wonderful set of research associates who contributed to the publication of more than thirty-five Contingency Planning Memoranda and helped produce the list of U.S. foreign policy crises included in this compilation. In chronological order, they are Jamie Ekern, Elise Vaughan, Sophia Yang, Steve Wittels, Andrew Miller, Alex Noyes, Rebecca Friedman-Lissner, Amelia Wolf, Helia Hock, Anna Feuer, Sarah Collman, James West, Jennifer Wilson, Megan Geckle, and Ellie Estreich. Various interns for the Center for Preventive Action, notably Jared Wright, Olivia McCoy, Katherine Donovan, Sara Sirota, Nilaya Knafo, and Jonah Glick-Unterman, also deserve mention for their help.

I would like to extend a profound thank you to all Contingency Planning Memoranda authors over the years as well. Their work has helped give concrete meaning to the importance of contingency planning and provided the impetus for this report.

Finally, this compilation would not have been possible without the financial support of the Rockefeller Brothers Fund of New York. For this, we are immensely grateful.

Paul B. Stares

ABOUT THE AUTHOR

Paul B. Stares is the General John W. Vessey senior fellow for conflict prevention and director of the Center for Preventive Action at the Council on Foreign Relations. An expert on conflict prevention and a regular commentator on current affairs, he is the author or editor of nine books on U.S. security policy and international relations. His latest book, *Preventive Engagement: How America Can Avoid War, Stay Strong, and Keep the Peace*, provides a blueprint for how the United States can manage a more turbulent and dangerous world. Prior to joining CFR, Stares was vice president and director of the Center for Conflict Analysis and Prevention at the U.S. Institute of Peace. He worked as associate director and senior research scholar at Stanford University's Center for International Security and Cooperation from 2000 to 2002 and was senior research fellow at the Japan Institute of International Affairs and then director of studies at the Japan Center for International Exchange from 1996 to 2000. He has also been a NATO fellow and a scholar in residence at the MacArthur Foundation's Moscow office. Stares has a BA from North Staffordshire Polytechnic and an MA and a PhD from Lancaster University.

ABOUT THE CENTER FOR PREVENTIVE ACTION

The Center for Preventive Action (CPA) seeks to help prevent, defuse, or resolve deadly conflicts around the world and to expand the body of knowledge on conflict prevention. It does so by creating a forum in which representatives of governments, international organizations, nongovernmental organizations, corporations, and civil society can gather to develop operational and timely strategies for promoting peace in specific conflict situations. The center focuses on conflicts in countries or regions that affect U.S. interests, but may be otherwise overlooked; where prevention appears possible; and when the resources of the Council on Foreign Relations can make a difference. The center does this by

- issuing regular reports to evaluate and respond rapidly to developing sources of instability and formulate timely, concrete policy recommendations that the U.S. government, international community, and local actors can use to limit the potential for deadly violence;

- engaging the U.S. government and news media in conflict prevention efforts. CPA staff members meet with administration officials and members of Congress to brief on CPA's findings and recommendations, facilitate contacts between U.S. officials and important local and external actors, and raise awareness among journalists of potential flashpoints around the globe;

- building networks with international organizations and institutions to complement and leverage the Council's established influence in the U.S. policy arena and increase the impact of CPA's recommendations; and

- providing a source of expertise on conflict prevention to include research, case studies, and lessons learned from past conflicts that policymakers and private citizens can use to prevent or mitigate future deadly conflicts.